SPELLING, PUNCTUATION & GRAMMAR

REVISION AND EXAM PRACTICE

ELIZABETH WALTER AND KATE WOODFORD

YORK PRESS
322 Old Brompton Road, London SW5 9JH

PEARSON EDUCATION LIMITED
Edinburgh Gate, Harlow,
Essex CM20 2JE, United Kingdom
Associated companies, branches and representatives throughout the world

First published 2017

10 9 8 7 6 5 4 3 2

ISBN 978–1–2921–8631–3

Phototypeset by Carnegie Book Production
Printed in Slovakia

Text credit: Extract from 'Singh Song!' from *Look We Have Coming to Dover!* by Daljit Nagra reproduced by permission of Faber and Faber Ltd.

Photo credits: percom/Shutterstock for page 5 bottom / Liza54500/Shutterstock for page 6 top and middle/ MAHATHIR MOHD YASIN/Shutterstock for page 6 top / Valentyn Volkov/Shutterstock for page 6 middle / Tatniz/© iStock for page 6 middle / Smolaw/Shuttertsock for page 7 bottom / copyright Jo Kemp for page 8 top / LuckyBusiness/© iStock for page 11 bottom / Africa Studio/Shutterstock for page 14 bottom / Mihai Simonia/Shutterstock for page 16 bottom / Vitchanan photography/Shutterstock for page 18 middle / Phovoir/Shutterstock for page 19 bottom / J. Bicking/Shuttertsock for page 21 middle / Suwanmanee99/© iStock for page 22 bottom / Vladimir Chernyanskiy/Shutterstock for page 23 top / oranoot/Shuttertsock for page 24 top / Nadina/Shuttertsock for page 25 bottom / Vibrant Image Studio/Shutterstock for page 31 bottom / kodachrome25/© iStock for page 33 bottom / Nolleks86/ Shutterstock for page 38 bottom / Highwaystarz-Photogrpahy/© iStock for page 40 bottom / AlinaMD/© iStock for page 42 middle / mennovandijk/© iStock for page 44 middle / epicurean/© iStock for page 44 bottom / Everett Collection/Shutterstock for page 48 middle / Hollygraphic/Shutterstock for page 49 top / Michaeljung/Shutterstock for page 50 bottom / Kosmos111/Shutterstock for page 52 bottom / Myronovych/Shutterstock for page 54 bottom / Pete Burana/Shutterstock for page 57 bottom / Kichigin/Shutterstock for page 59 middle / Kurhan/Shutterstock for page 63 middle / Hung Chung Chih/Shutterstock for page 64 bottom / Yiorgos GR/Shutterstock for page 67 bottom / Michaeljung/ Shutterstock for page 69 top

CONTENTS

INTRODUCTION: WHY YOU NEED TO MAKE SURE YOUR SPaG IS UP TO STANDARD

PART ONE: HOW GOOD IS YOUR SPaG?

PART TWO: SPELLINGS FOR SUCCESS

PART THREE: GET YOUR GRAMMAR RIGHT!

PART FOUR: PUNCTUATION FOR ACCURACY AND EFFECT

PART FIVE: PARAGRAPHS AND ORGANISATION

PART SIX: TEST YOURSELF

PART SEVEN: ANSWERS AND GLOSSARY

WHAT IS SPAG AND WHY IS IT SO IMPORTANT?

SPaG is a useful acronym that stands for 'Spelling, Punctuation and Grammar'. It may not be the most exciting of subjects, but it is undeniably important. There are several reasons for this:

- In a number of GCSE subjects, especially **English Language**, you will gain marks for the correct use of spelling, punctuation and grammar (see page 7 for information on marks). You will lose marks for incorrect use, so it is worth devoting some time to this subject.
- Some of the **rules** governing spelling, punctuation and grammar are tricky, but many are not and can be learnt with a little application. Once you understand these rules, they will help you to **pick up marks in your exams** – or at least ensure that you do not lose marks.
- When **writing essays**, you may have all the facts at your fingertips, and your ideas and insights may be perfectly valid, but if you cannot convey those points in a way that is clear and concise, your grades might disappoint you. A good grasp of spelling, punctuation and grammar will ensure that the points you make can be understood by the examiner.
- A good knowledge of SPaG will serve you well in the longer term, too, whether you are applying for a **university course or a job**. It will also help greatly when you are in employment, as so much work requires **written communication**. Beyond college and work, the ability to use language well in both speech and writing will give you greater **confidence** in expressing yourself. It also helps to ensure that your ideas come across successfully, making communication more precise and effective.

SPELLING

Spelling in English can be challenging. Sometimes it is hard to remember whether a word has one consonant or two. Likewise, you may forget the order in which the vowels of a word appear. To make matters worse, there are a number of English words that sound the same but are spelt differently and have different meanings – for example the verb **'affect'** and the noun **'effect'**. Many of these are words that you will need to use in your GCSE exams. You will not be able to take a dictionary or hand-held device into the exam room, so you will need to learn the spellings beforehand.

Away from the exam room, computer spell checkers and grammar checkers are useful but they will not always help to fix your errors. For example, a spell checker might not pick up on the fact that the wrong verb ('bare') has been used in the following sentence:

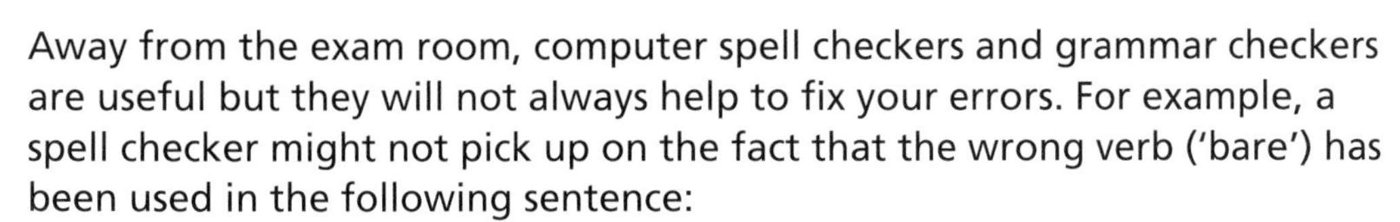

*At times, the sadness was too much to **bare**.* ×

*At times, the sadness was too much to **bear**.* ✓

Again, the only way to avoid this happening is to be aware of such spelling pitfalls and to make a determined effort to memorise any that are likely to catch you out.

PUNCTUATION

Punctuation performs an essential function in writing. It makes the meaning of written language clear and unambiguous. Consider the following two sentences:

I helped, Jamie.

I helped Jamie.

In the first sentence, the speaker is clearly addressing Jamie and in the second, they are relating that they assisted Jamie in some way. The addition of a comma creates a very different meaning.

Maria brought ice cream and fruit.

Maria brought ice, cream and fruit.

How many items did Maria bring: two or three? Clearly, punctuation is important. Good punctuation ensures that the message intended by the writer is conveyed successfully to the reader.

GRAMMAR

Grammar refers to the structure of a language and the rules that govern the way words fit together. It is possible to speak quite well with very little knowledge of grammar, but in order to write clear, correct English, it is important to have a basic knowledge of the rules. For example, you may hear people say 'we was', 'you was' or 'they was', but this is not standard English grammar and should never be used in a written exam.

An additional benefit of having a good grasp of English grammar is that it is extremely helpful when learning a second language.

SPAG FOR GCSE ENGLISH LANGUAGE

More than any other GCSE subject, English Language requires a thorough knowledge of SPaG. It accounts for **40 per cent** of the written mark in English Language and **20 per cent** of the overall grade, including Reading and Writing. In this exam, you will need to demonstrate your understanding of several key aspects of spelling, punctuation and grammar, all of which are covered in this book. You will need to prove that you can:

- Spell accurately
- Make correct use of punctuation
- Write English that is grammatically correct
- Use a range of interesting vocabulary, allowing for clear and precise expression
- Employ varied sentence structures and types in order to achieve different effects
- Organise your thoughts and ideas into sensible paragraphs, using appropriate linking devices

SPAG FOR GCSE ENGLISH LITERATURE

Although the focus of this exam is the analysis of literature rather than language, all the above points for GCSE English Language are valid. Bear in mind that **5 per cent** of marks are specifically awarded for spelling, punctuation and grammar (for certain texts only).

In addition, in order to analyse the writing of other authors, you will need to have a good grasp of the following:

- The language features and techniques that writers use in order to convey **mood**, **tone**, emotion, etc.
- The correct terminology to describe those features and techniques

SPAG FOR OTHER GCSE SUBJECTS

Five per cent of the overall marks in a number of GCSE subjects (currently Geography, History and Religious Studies) are allocated for spelling, punctuation and grammar. Furthermore, poor SPaG might mean that you fail to convey valid information to the examiner. In other words, whatever the subject, you need to know your SPaG! This book focuses primarily on spelling, punctuation and grammar for GCSE English Language and Literature, but the information and techniques provided here will benefit you when you are studying and taking exams for other subjects.

SPAG CHECK

Work through these questions to find out how good you are at spelling, punctuation and grammar. Score yourself against the answers on pages 12–13, then use the 'How did you do?' section on page 14 to discover how you can use this book to help you improve.

1 Circle the correct **spelling**.

a) *The story is set in the* [desert / dessert] *of Arizona.*

b) *He can no longer deny the* [existence / existance] *of these feelings.*

c) *Her moods are* [changeable / changable] *and unpredictable.*

d) *His* [tendancy / tendency] *to cry irritates her.*

e) *This is a moral* [dilema / dilemma] *for Karl.*

f) *His* [apparent / apparant] *indifference to her plight is shocking.*

g) *There was a sudden flash of* [lightening / lightning].

h) [Admitedly / Admittedly], *this situation is far from ideal.*

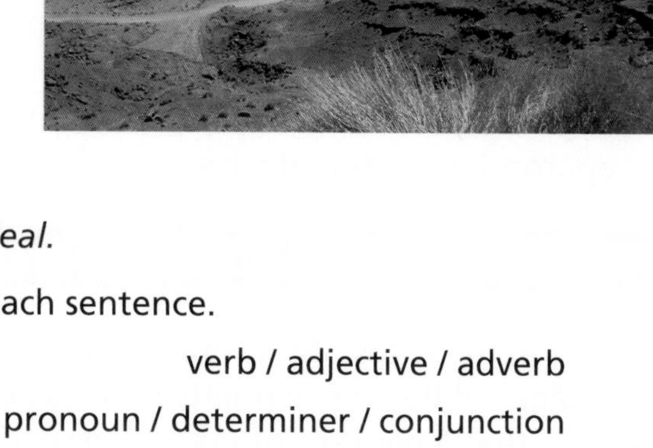

2 Circle the correct **word class** of the underlined word in each sentence.

a) *He walked wearily to the car.*	verb / adjective / adverb
b) *They were leaving the house when it happened.*	pronoun / determiner / conjunction
c) *Through the mist, she perceived a figure in the distance.*	noun / verb / adjective
d) *The storm lasted for several hours.*	determiner / preposition / conjunction
e) *The child's eyes were the most exquisite shade of blue.*	verb / adjective / adverb
f) *Sue was afraid, although she was with friends.*	determiner / preposition / conjunction
g) *Sajid rarely raised his voice.*	verb / adjective / adverb
h) *They took shelter under a tree.*	determiner / preposition / conjunction

3 Match the **sentence** with the sentence **type**. (There is one of each.)

a) Good morning!
b) He left the house although she begged him not to.
c) We got in the car and we drove.
d) The door slammed shut.

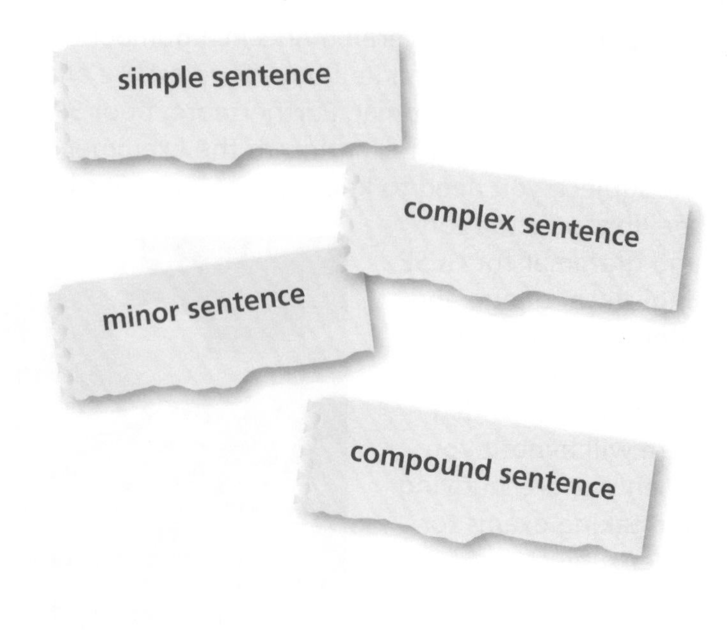

4 Indicate whether these are **concrete nouns** (C), **abstract nouns** (A), or **proper nouns** (P).

a) Shakespeare [ ]
b) banana [ ]
c) childhood [ ]
d) Taj Mahal [ ]
e) misery [ ]
f) apartment [ ]
g) country [ ]
h) California [ ]
i) confusion [ ]
j) appetite [ ]

5 Is the form of the underlined verb in these sentences correct (✓) or incorrect (×)? If incorrect, provide the correct form.

a) *How has the poet used imagery to convey his sadness?* ❑ ....
b) *One of his later novels are set in Ireland.* ❑ ....
c) *Julia and her daughter, Nina, are devastated by the news.* ❑ ....
d) *One of these earlier poems deals with the same theme.* ❑ ....
e) *How does Ben and his sister respond to the news?* ❑ ....

6 Complete these sentences with the correct **past participle** of the **irregular verbs** in brackets.

a) *She had already* .... (show) *her mother the photograph.*

b) *The night air was cold and a light snow had* .... (begin) *to fall.*

c) *He had* .... (wake) *early, with the first light.*

d) *The pain was terrible and could not be* .... (bear).

e) *His mother had cried and* .... (wring) *her hands on hearing the news.*

f) *Seeing Anya at the door, Mark had* .... (spring) *to his feet.*

g) *He walked disconsolately around the neighbourhood that he had long* .... (outgrow).

h) *Kyra had tried to embrace him but he had* .... (shake) *her off.*

i) *He had* .... (swear) *blind that he was innocent.*

j) *Katie had fallen and* .... (tear) *her skirt.*

7 Decide whether these **adjectives** used to describe sound are usually seen as positive (P), negative (N) or neutral (X).

a) melodic [ ]
b) shrill [ ]
c) grating [ ]
d) deafening [ ]
e) loud [ ]
f) mellow [ ]
g) piercing [ ]
h) low [ ]

8 Add **commas** in the correct place in these sentences.

a) *Likewise young people should not immediately dismiss the opinions of the older people.*

b) *Macbeth who has an extremely vivid imagination finds himself in the grip of almost hallucinatory visions.*

c) *We entered a long dark room.*

d) *You didn't see Eleanor did you?*

e) *I have something to tell you Luke.*

f) *Even though she was devoted to her family she still found time to write.*

9 Is the use of **apostrophes** (') in these sentences correct (✓) or incorrect (×)? If incorrect, write them out correctly.

a) *Her whole life was devoted to promoting womens' rights.* ☐ ....

b) *I'd never met Charles's wife so was interested to see what she was like.* ☐ ....

c) *Whatever our opinion of him, the fact remains that he is the people's choice of leader.* ☐ ....

d) *The room was full of pianos'.* ☐ ....

e) *She's very interested in the fashions of the '50s.* ☐ ....

f) *They could imitate each others' voices.* ☐ ....

g) *For years to come, I would remember the child's expression.* ☐ ....

h) *The soldiers' uniforms were infested with lice.* ☐ ....

10 Add **inverted commas** and any other punctuation to these sentences where it is needed.

a) *Where did Joe go she asked.*

b) *The child explained that she was looking for her mother.*

c) *He replied I have no idea.*

d) *She added that she too was feeling guilty.*

11 Circle the **connective** that works better in each of these sentences.

a) *Children respond well to praise from their parents.* [Similarly / On the other hand], *they react well to positive feedback from teachers.*

b) *A number of patients with the disease had not been diagnosed.* [In other words / Conversely], *a small number of people who didn't have the disease had been wrongly diagnosed with it.*

c) *Teenagers have nowhere to go in the evening and* [above all / consequently] *resort to socialising in public places, such as parks and bus shelters.*

d) *Despite millions of pounds being spent on public information campaigns, we continue to eat unhealthily.* [In other words / For instance], *education is not working.*

e) *On average, 40 per cent of people in this country do not vote.* [Evidently / To this end], *a large proportion of the population feels completely disengaged from the democratic process.*

⓬ Read the following English Language GCSE exam-style question and then proofread the extract from a student's answer. There are **eight** errors in the spelling, punctuation and grammar.

> *'School summer holidays are too long. Most students get bored as the weeks drag on and they forget much of what they have learnt. Students should spend more time at school.'*
>
> *Write an article for a broadsheet newspaper in which you explain your point of view on this statement.*

All through the school year, teenagers like me work hard for weeks on end. Its a dull routine consisting of the same tedious lessons but I willingly put up with it, the reason for that is that I always have the long summer break to look forward to. However, some interfering adults have started suggesting that the summer holidays are to long. Instead of enjoying the summer months relaxing, they want me to spend even more long slogging away at school because English Maths and Science are vital for my future. Yes, I know these subjects are important but I might enjoy them more if I am given a brake from them sometimes!

Who says that the summer holidays make kids bored. I'm never bored for a moment! Perhaps a few people get restless in the summer but I happen to think that holidays are an important part of my education. When I meet my friends in town for coffee or a shopping trip we chat all the time. Consequently my social skills improve. I get very little opportunity to practise like that in school. If I start talking to friends in a lesson, a teacher soon puts an end to our discussions.

Now check your answers against those on pages 12–13. Turn to page 14 for advice on using this book to improve your knowledge of SPaG.

Now check how you did and then look at the marks grid for suggested follow-up.

ANSWERS

1

a) desert

b) existence

c) changeable

d) tendency

e) dilemma

f) apparent

g) lightning

h) Admittedly

2

a) adverb

b) pronoun

c) verb

d) determiner

e) adjective

f) conjunction

g) adverb

h) preposition

3

a) minor sentence

b) complex sentence

c) compound sentence

d) simple sentence

4

a) P

b) C

c) A

d) P

e) A

f) C

g) C

h) P

i) A

j) A

5

a) ✓

b) × (is)

c) ✓

d) ✓

e) × (do)

6

a) shown

b) begun

c) woken

d) borne

e) wrung

f) sprung

g) outgrown

h) shaken

i) sworn

j) torn

7

a) 1

b) 2

c) 2

d) 2

e) 3

f) 1

g) 2

h) 3

8

a) Likewise, young people …

b) Macbeth, who has an extremely vivid imagination, finds himself in the grip of almost hallucinatory visions.

c) We entered a long, dark room.

d) You didn't see Eleanor, did you?

e) I have something to tell you, Luke.

f) Even though she was devoted to her family, she still found time to write.

9

a) × (women's)

b) ✓

c) ✓

d) × (pianos)

e) ✓

f) × (other's)

g) ✓

h) ✓

10

a) 'Where did Joe go**?'** she asked.

b) The child explained that she was looking for her mother. (no change)

c) He replied**, '**I have no idea.'

d) She added that she too was feeling guilty. (no change)

11

a) Similarly

b) Conversely

c) consequently

d) In other words

e) Evidently

12

All through the school year, teenagers like me work hard for weeks on end. ***Its*** *[1] a dull routine consisting of the same tedious lessons but I willingly put up with it****,*** *[2] the reason for that is that I always have the long summer break to look forward to. However, some interfering adults have started suggesting that the summer holidays are* ***to*** *[3] long. Instead of enjoying the summer months relaxing, they want me to spend even more* ***long*** *[4] slogging away at school because* ***English Maths and Science*** *[5] are vital for my future. Yes, I know these subjects are important but I might enjoy them more if I am given a* ***brake*** *[6] from them sometimes!*

Who says that the summer holidays make kids bored. [7] I'm never bored for a moment! Perhaps a few people get restless in the summer but I happen to think that holidays are an important part of my education. When I meet my friends in town for coffee or a shopping trip we chat all the time. ***Consequently*** *[8] my social skills improve. I get very little opportunity to practise like that in school. If I start talking to friends in a lesson, a teacher soon puts an end to our discussions.*

Comments on SPaG errors

[1] The student should have written 'It is' or used the contracted form 'It's'. Instead they have mistakenly used the possessive **determiner** 'its' (this has been used correctly in sentences such as 'The cat had hurt its leg' and 'The region has its own identity').

[2] A new sentence is needed here. The student has mistakenly run two sentences together, making a mistake known as a **comma splice**.

[3] The adverb 'too' is needed here, meaning 'excessively'. The student has confused this word with the common **preposition** 'to'.

[4] The student should have written 'longer' (without 'more'). **Adjectives** such as 'long' that have one syllable usually form their **comparatives** by adding '-er'.

[5] A comma is needed here between the words 'English' and 'Maths'. Commas are used to separate items in a list of three or more people or things. Generally, in a list like this, a comma is not needed before 'and'.

[6] The noun that the student intended here, meaning a period of rest, is 'break'. This noun ('brake') refers to the device that makes a vehicle slow down.

[7] A question mark ('?') is needed at the end of this **rhetorical question**, rather than a full stop.

[8] A comma is missing here. When adverbs such as 'Moreover', 'Similarly' and 'Consequently' start a sentence, they should be followed by a comma.

HOW DID YOU DO?

Give yourself one mark for each correct answer to come up with a total out of 84 to assess your SPaG skills. Follow the advice in the table below to improve your skills, working on the areas that require most improvement.

Total mark .... [out of 84]

Your mark	Suggested steps to take

0–20 marks	• Work through Part One to Part Five of this book carefully, without skipping any parts.
	• Do all the tasks and if your score is lower than you hoped in any of them, go back to the relevant spelling, grammar or punctuation point in the book and try to improve your understanding of it:
	  • Need help with spelling? Go to page 15.
	  • Struggling with grammar? Go to page 30.
	  • Want to practise your punctuation? Go to page 48.
	  • Improve your paragraphing and organisation? Go to page 62.
	• To see how your understanding has improved, allow a day or two to pass and then revisit the tasks in the question. Once you are satisfied that you have a good grasp of all the areas, do Part Six: 'Test yourself'.

20–50 marks	• Highlight the exercises in which you did not score so well and start by studying these areas in the book. Set aside a day to focus on them, making sure that you do the relevant tasks. • When you have completed that phase, go back to the beginning of the book and work through all the other areas, making sure that you have a firm grasp of them. • Once you are confident that you understand all the sections in the book, do Part Six: 'Test yourself'.
50–84 marks	• Highlight any exercises in which you scored less than 100 per cent and focus specifically on these. • Go straight to the relevant areas of the book, making sure that you do any tasks that are provided. • When you have done this, go back to the beginning of the book and read it quickly from beginning to end. • This will consolidate your understanding of the more difficult areas and perhaps teach you some terminology you did not know before. Then do Part Six: 'Test yourself'.

SPELLING STRATEGIES

English spelling can be challenging. With many other languages, the spelling of a word can be guessed accurately from the way the word sounds. This is not always the case for English words, so it is useful to learn strategies to master difficult spellings. Choose the strategy that works best for you.

STRATEGY 1: 'LOOK, SAY, COVER, WRITE, CHECK'

Some people find it helpful to learn a spelling by breaking down the task into five steps:

- **Look** carefully at the word. Pay particular attention to any difficult parts, highlighting them if it helps.
- **Say** the word aloud. Listen to how it sounds.
- **Cover** the word. Now try to visualise the letters.
- **Write** the word.
- **Check** what you have written. Did you get it right? If not, try again.

STRATEGY 2: MNEMONICS

A **mnemonic** (do not pronounce the first 'm'!) is a memorable phrase or sentence that helps you to remember something. Mnemonics are a great tool for learning difficult spellings. They work in different ways.

They may help you remember the difficult letters in a word that can catch you out. For example, a mnemonic may help you remember the correct vowel or the correct order of two vowels:

*There's a **sin** in bu**sin**ess.*

*Never bel**ie**ve a **lie**.*

***We** are **we**ird.*

Mnemonics may help you spell out a whole word. In this type of mnemonic, the first letters of each word in a sentence form the challenging word:

***B**ig **e**lephants **c**an't **a**lways **u**nderstand **s**mall **e**lephants. = because*

***N**ever **e**at **c**hocolate – **e**at **s**pinach **s**alad **a**nd **r**emain **y**oung. = necessary*

Mnemonics may help you remember which of two similarly spelt words is which:

desert v dessert *There's an extra 's' in dessert because it's extra **s**weet.*

stationery v stationary *Stationery helps you to write l**e**tters.*

1. Make up a mnemonic to help you remember one of the spellings below that you find tricky.

relevant	perceive	achieve	humorous	precede	gauge

STRATEGY 3: WORDS INSIDE WORDS

Sometimes, the difficult parts of words are words themselves. It can help your spelling if you memorise the short words inside the longer words – for example:

accept**able**	exis**ten**ce	pri**vile**ge
address	fami**liar**	relev**ant**
appa**rent**	hier**arch**y	separ**ate**
ar**gum**ent	indepen**dent**	
envi**iron**ment	persis**tent**	

STRATEGY 4: SYLLABLES AND WORD-SPLITTING

Another way to learn the spelling of a word is to break it up, either into **syllables** or into 'parts', and then say them out loud. This works well for words that are not spelt as they are said – for example:

Wed + nes + day

bus + in + ess

ce + met + er + y

ec + sta + sy

en + vi + ron + ment

go + vern + ment

li + ai + son

ten + den + cy

TOP TIP

Reading is hugely enjoyable and beneficial in many ways, but it will not automatically improve your spelling. If you know you are going to need to write a word with complex spelling, make an effort to learn it.

❷ Choose ten spellings from the box below that you cannot confidently spell and choose one of the strategies above to learn them.

accommodation	exceed	omission
acknowledge	exhilarating	outrageous
acquire	existence	parliament
changeable	fascinating	possession
committed	foreign	surprise
conscientious	fulfil	tyranny
conscious	lightning	vicious
dilemma	miniature	withhold
disappointed	occasion	
embarrassed	occurrence	

TOP TIP

Keep a customised list of any words that you struggle to spell and make repeated efforts to master them.

USEFUL WORDS FOR ENGLISH ESSAYS

The lists on these pages contain words that you will need to use in English essays. All have difficult spellings, so make sure you know them.

Adjectives and nouns used for English Literature and Language essays:

Word	Definition
allegory	a story that can be interpreted to reveal a hidden meaning
anonymous	something that is not identified by a name
antithesis	the direct opposite of something
assonance	when two or more words near each other have the same vowel sound
character	a person who appears in a work of fiction
chronological	when events are described in the order in which they occurred
colloquial	everyday speech used by people in ordinary situations
conscious	aware of
contemporary	describing things that live at the same time
denouement	the final part of a story, play or film
dialogue	speech and conversation between characters
dissonance	lack of agreement or harmony
euphemism	a word or phrase used in place of others if they are considered too harsh or embarrassing
figurative	words or phrases used to express a meaning that is different to their literal meaning
foreboding	a sense that something bad is going to happen
genre	a type of story, based on its style (e.g. horror, science fiction, romance)
hyperbole	exaggerated statements that are not meant to be taken literally
malevolent	evil
metaphor	when one thing is used to describe another to create a striking or unusual image
monologue	a long speech by a character in a play

Word	Definition
narrative	a spoken or written account of events
narrator	the person who gives a spoken or written account of events
omniscient	knowing everything
onomatopoeia	a word that suggests its meaning through its sound
onomatopoeic	describing something that suggests its meaning through its sound
oxymoron	a figure of speech that uses apparently contradictory words in conjunction for effect (e.g. same difference)
pastiche	a work that imitates another
personification	describing an object or idea as though it was human, with feelings and attributes
playwright	someone who writes plays
protagonist	the main or a major character
psychology	the scientific study of the human mind
reference	mentioning something else
repetition	the act of saying something that has already been said
rhetorical	not requiring an answer
rhyme	the same sound in words or the end of words, particularly at the end of lines of poetry
rhythm	a strong repeated pattern
simile	when one thing is compared directly with another using 'as' or 'like'
soliloquy	a dramatic technique that allows a character to speak as if thinking aloud
speech	words spoken aloud
syllable	one of the parts into which a word can be divided
technique	a method of doing something

❸ Highlight the words in this list that you find difficult to spell, and use a strategy to remember them. Come back to this list later and test yourself on the spellings.

Words and phrases that are useful for analysis and expressing opinions:

additionally	doubt	notably
admittedly	furthermore	opinion
advocate	however	opposed
analogous	in practice	parallel
believe	in spite of	particularly
comparable	issue	perspective
concur	maintain	similarly
consequence	moreover	therefore
consequently	nevertheless	undoubtedly
contradict	nonetheless	whereas

CHECK YOUR SKILLS

4. Find any spelling errors in these sentences and then write the sentences correctly on a separate sheet of paper.

   a) *At the same time, the repitition of the vowels 'a' and 'e' gives rise to assanance, which heightens this effect.*
   b) *Many of the poem's metaphors and similies reflect the same theme.*
   c) *Admitedly, there is a problem in our society that needs addressing.*
   d) *This is undoutedly particularly true of people of retirement age.*
   e) *There is a great deal of pathos in the novel, most noteably in the depiction of the narrater's ageing parents.*
   f) *This is one of two main soliloqueys delivered by the protaganist.*
   g) *Furthermore, some even claim that these two principles contredict each other.*
   h) *These are issues that primarily affect young people and they are therefor more likely to engage with them.*
   i) *Swain uses similar imagery later in the chapter, complaining that being in debt is analagous to having a noose around his neck.*
   j) *The 'gathering clouds' and 'darkening skies' in the opening paragraph create a sense of forboding.*

LETTER ORDER AND SILENT LETTERS

Sometimes you will simply need to learn the spellings of difficult words such as those with silent letters. However, there are some ways of remembering the order of letters in certain words.

THE 'I' BEFORE 'E' RULE

If you are unsure whether to write 'ie' or 'ei' in a word, there is a useful **mnemonic** to remember:

'i' before 'e', except after 'c'.

In other words, write 'ie' except when the letter before those two letters is 'c', in which case write 'ei' – for example:

'I' before 'e': ac**hie**ve, b**rie**f, c**hie**f, f**rie**nd, **pie**ce, sh**rie**k

except after 'c': **cei**ling, con**cei**ted, per**cei**ve, re**cei**ve

However, there is a second part to this mnemonic:

'I' before 'e', except after 'c', *but only when it makes the sound 'ee'*.

In other words, this rule does not apply when the letters 'i' and 'e' combine to make a sound that is not 'ee' – for example:

an**cie**nt, cons**cie**nce, effi**cie**nt, s**cie**nce, so**cie**ty, suffi**cie**nt
beige, f**ei**gn, f**ei**sty, for**ei**gn, h**ei**r, l**ei**sure, n**ei**ghbour, th**ei**r, w**ei**ght

There are a few exceptions to the 'i' before 'e' rule, where the sound made by the two vowels is 'ee' but the rules outlined above do not apply. If you know you will need to write these words, it is a good idea simply to learn them – for example:

spe**cie**s
caff**ei**ne, prot**ei**n, s**ei**ze, w**ei**rd

1. Are the vowels 'e' and 'i' in the correct order in these words? If they are incorrect, write down the correct spelling.

   a) acheive ....
   b) friend ....
   c) recieve ....
   d) perceive ....
   e) efficient ....
   f) foriegn ....
   g) species ....
   h) weight ....
   i) protien ....
   j) weird ....

SILENT LETTERS

Some words contain letters that are not pronounced. When you cannot hear a letter as you are saying the word, it is an easy mistake to leave that letter out when writing it. Make an effort to learn the spellings of these common words with silent letters.

Words with a silent 'b':

bomb
climb
debt
doubt
numb
subtle
succumb
tomb

Words with a silent 'c':

conscience
conscious
descend
fascinating
scenario
scene
science

Words with a silent 'g':

campaign
design
feign
foreign
reign
sign

Words with a silent 'h':

ghost
rhyme
whale
wheel
where
which
white
whisper

Words with a silent 'k':

knee
kneel
knife
knock
knot
know
knowledge

Words with a silent 'l':

calm
could
half
should
would

Words with a silent 't':

bustle
castle
fasten
glisten
listen
rustle
soften
whistle

Words with a silent 'w':

answer
playwright
sword
whole
wreak

❷ These sentences each contain a word that is missing a silent letter.
Circle the words with the missing letter, then write the correct spelling.

a) *They were both playrights in the eighteenth century.* ....

b) *She describes the 'not of anxiety' in her stomach.* ....

c) *The hole tone of the paragraph is pessimistic.* ....

d) *In the distance, someone whisles tunelessly.* ....

e) *The ryme of the poem is irregular, almost random.* ....

f) *She describes the busle of the busy marketplace.* ....

g) *She was devastated, num with grief.* ....

❸ These sentences are all missing a word that uses a silent letter.
Write the missing word.

a) *The storm had .... havoc, bringing trees and fences down and scattering rubbish everywhere.*

b) *Local people have launched a .... to stop the development on the plot.*

c) *Alone in the cemetery, she .... down to place the flowers.*

d) *There's no anaesthetic used. The patient remains .... throughout the operation.*

e) *Her .... of the subject is quite extensive.*

f) *We are introduced to both the main characters in the play's opening ....*

g) *The leaves in the trees .... gently in the breeze.*

h) *Today marks the beginning of the election ....*

i) *The King stepped down after a forty-year ....*

i) *Christopher Marlowe, the .... , lived at the same time as Shakespeare.*

UNDERSTANDING PLURALS

Plural forms can be challenging, but there are some rules you can follow to get them right.

PLURAL FORMS WITH '-ES'

To make most nouns plural, simply add '-s' to the end.

thing → things

base → bases

However, for words ending in the letters 's', 'x', 'z', 'sh' or 'ch', add '-es' to make them plural:

box → boxes

branch → branches

bus → buses

gas → gases

dish → dishes

dress → dresses

tax → taxes

wish → wishes

TOP TIP

If you have written a plural noun and it looks impossible to say, consider whether you should replace the '-s' on the end with '-es' – for example, churchs (×) churches (✓).

PLURAL FORMS WITH '-IES'

If a word ends in a consonant plus 'y' (for example, 'story', 'spy'), make it plural by replacing the 'y' with 'i' and adding the letters '-es'.

country → countries

fly → flies

memory → memories

quality → qualities

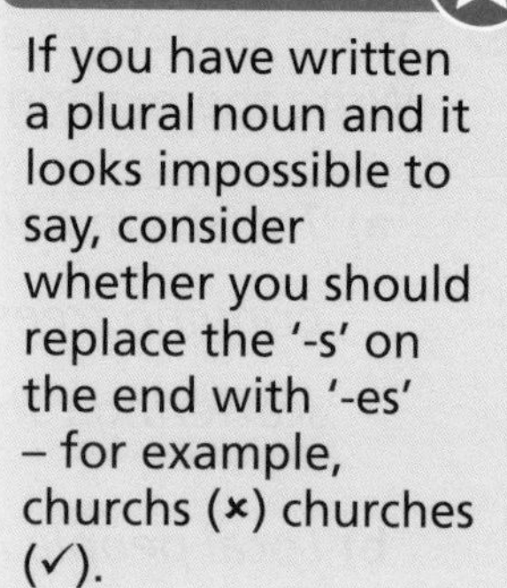

However, note that this rule does not apply to people's names:

*The Kenne**dys** were at the protest.*

*Did you see the Krishnamur**thys** there?*

*Both Hol**lys** have been invited – Smith and Taylor.*

WORDS ENDING IN 'O'

To make a plural of a word that ends in 'o', you usually add '-s' (for example, 'kilos', 'memos'). A small set of words ending in '-o' require '-es' on the end. Unfortunately, there is no rule to help you remember these '-oes' plurals. You simply have to learn them.

*domin**oes***	*her**oes***	*tomat**oes***
*ech**oes***	*potat**oes***	*vet**oes***

WORDS ENDING IN 'F' AND 'FE'

To make a plural of a word that ends in 'f' or 'fe', change the 'f' or 'fe' to 'v' and add '-es'.

half → halves

calf → calves

knife → knives

leaf → leaves

life → lives

loaf → loaves

scarf → scarves

wolf → wolves

Again, there are a few exceptions to this rule, and you simply have to learn them:

belief → beliefs

chef → chefs

reef → reefs

roof → roofs

PLURAL FORMS THAT ARE THE SAME

A small number of nouns have a plural form that is the same as the singular form.

TOP TIP 

Note that 'fishes' is sometimes used as the plural form to refer to different species of fish.

They include some animals:

buffalo → buffalo

deer → deer

fish → fish

moose → moose

sheep → sheep

They also include words that end in 'craft':

aircraft → aircraft

spacecraft → spacecraft

Some words that end in 'ies' also have a plural form that is the same as the singular form:

series → series

species → species

IRREGULAR PLURAL FORMS

Some words have an irregular plural form that does not follow the usual rules. Many of these words are used frequently in science subjects, so it is worth learning them:

analysis → analyses

antenna → antennae or antennas

antithesis → antitheses

bacterium → bacteria

basis → bases

cactus → cacti or cactuses

crisis → crises

criterion → criteria

diagnosis → diagnoses

formula → formulae or formulas

fungus → fungi or funguses

larva → larvae or larvas

parenthesis → parentheses

phenomenon → phenomena

stimulus → stimuli

woman → women

1. Find the incorrectly spelt forms in this excerpt from a student's creative writing piece. Write the correct forms on a separate piece of paper.

It was seven o'clock in the morning and bitterly cold when Rebecca set off. She turned left at the end of the road and walked towards the stream. The rooves of the houses that she passed sparkled with frost and the leafs under her feet crunched as she stepped on them. She loved this time of year. It brought back so many happy memorys of playing with her younger brother in the back garden, wrapped snuggly in scarfs, their cheeks as red as tomatos.

She thought of her brother, Ali, as she crossed the road to join the path beside the stream. They would come here in the summer, when the air was buzzing with flys. Ali used to love delving in the water with his net, trying – and always failing – to catch a fish. There were no fish this morning – they were presumably keeping warm at the bottom of the stream. The other side of the stream, there was a small wooded area. She would take her brother there, his plump, trusting hand in hers. Once, just once, she had told him that there were wolfs in the wood and he had cried and begged to be taken home. She hadn't meant to upset him, just to inject a little excitement into their walk.

COMMONLY CONFUSED WORDS

English has many words that sound the same but have quite different spellings and meanings. It is easy to confuse these words when writing. Try to memorise the differences between them.

ACCEPT VS EXCEPT

'Accept' is a verb. It has several meanings, such as to agree that something is true, and to say yes to an offer:

The theory is now widely accepted.

Reluctantly, she accepted the invitation.

'Except' means but not:

Everyone was present except the girl's father.

AFFECT VS EFFECT

'Affect' is a verb and 'effect' is a generally a noun. To 'affect' someone or something is to cause them to change in some way:

These policies affect every aspect of our lives.

An 'effect' is a change that has been caused:

Pollutants like these have a damaging effect on our health.

BARE VS BEAR

'Bare' is an **adjective** and means without clothes or empty. It is also used in phrases such as 'bare essentials' and 'bare minimum', meaning most basic:

The child, with her bare legs and arms, was evidently cold.

All he carried with him was a blanket and some water – the bare essentials.

'Bear' is a noun, referring to the large wild animal with thick fur. It is also a verb, meaning to put up with or accept something bad or difficult.

She couldn't bear to leave him.

The pressure on him is huge, but he bears it well.

BRAKE VS BREAK

A brake is a device that stops a moving vehicle. It is also a verb, meaning to cause a vehicle to stop moving:

She heard the screech of brakes as his car pulled up.

He braked sharply, causing the car to come to a standstill.

For all other senses, noun and verb, use 'break':

After three hours of digging, we took a short break.

She felt as if her heart would break.

He longed for a sound to break the silence.

GET IT RIGHT!

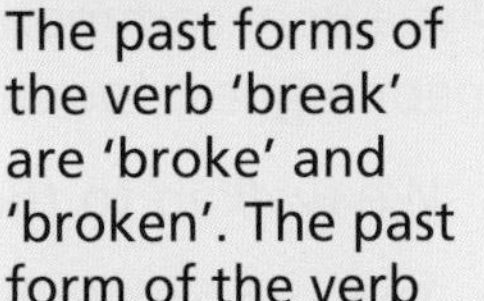

The past forms of the verb 'break' are 'broke' and 'broken'. The past form of the verb 'brake' is 'braked'.

LOOSE VS LOSE

'Lose' is a verb with several meanings, including to not win and to not now have something:

We might lose the match.

I'm always losing umbrellas!

'Loose' is an adjective, meaning not fixed or held in place:

He wore a loose-fitting sweater and jeans.

PAST VS PASSED

'Passed' is the past **tense** of the verb 'pass'. If you write that someone or something **does** something, you need this verb and **not** the word 'past':

Time had passed so slowly since that point.

Laws have been passed to restrict this practice.

I passed the note to Mira.

'Past' means 'beyond a certain point in time or place':

She looked at her watch – ten past four.

I walked past the church.

'Past' is also a noun and an **adjective**, referring to the time before the present:

In the past, children as young as six worked in these factories.

In the past ten years, this situation has changed.

GET IT RIGHT!

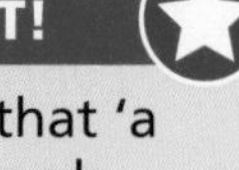

'Remember that 'a lot' is two words. Do not write it as one word.

A lot of people still believe this. ✓

Alot of people still believe this. ×

THAN VS THEN

'Than' is used only for comparisons:

He was taller than his father.

Surely happiness is more important than money?

'Then' is used for talking about time. It refers either to a particular point in the past or future, or it is used before saying the next thing that happens.

I'll see him after school and speak to him then.

We called in at the café and then came home.

TO VS TOO

'To' is a very common word in the English language, used to say where someone goes, for example, and to show the purpose of an action:

*We walked **to** the city centre **to** go to the cinema.*

They rushed to help the young woman.

'Too' is used before adjectives and **adverbs** to mean excessively:

It was too hot in the sun so we came indoors.

'Too' is also used to mean as well: *Maria was there and her daughter too.*

PREFIXES AND SUFFIXES

SPELLINGS WITH PREFIXES

Prefixes and **suffixes** are small groups of letters that are added to words to change their meaning. Prefixes (for example, 'pre-' and 'un-') are added to the beginnings of words. Suffixes (for example, '-ful' and '-less') are added to the ends of words.

When adding a prefix to a word, do not change the spelling of the original word:

cultural → multicultural *discover → rediscover*

interpret → misinterpret *usual → unusual*

When a prefix ending in 's' is added to a word that starts with 's', the new word contains 'ss':

mis + spell → misspell *dis + similar → dissimilar*

SPELLINGS WITH SUFFIXES

If the original word ends in 'e' and the suffix also starts with a vowel, leave out the 'e' in the original word:

hope + -ing → hoping *blue + ish → bluish*

If the suffix starts with a consonant, keep the 'e' in the original word:

bore + dom → boredom *rude + ness → rudeness*

When the original word is short (one **syllable**) and ends in a consonant, double the consonant when adding a suffix:

stop + ing → stopping *swim + er → swimmer*

Note that this rule does not apply when the original word ends in two consonants.

rank + ed → ranked *fling + ing → flinging*

GET IT RIGHT! 

Remember that the suffix '-ful' on the end of a word has only one 'l' (for example, 'beautiful', 'dreadful', 'hopeful').

CHECK YOUR SKILLS

1. Choose the correct spellings in these sentences.
   - a) *She suddenly let out a piercing* [shriek / shriek].
   - b) *He had been angry with her, called her* [concieted / conceited] *and vain.*
   - c) *Her mind was full of* [doubt / dout].
   - d) *It was rumoured that there were* [wolfs / wolves] *in the forest.*
   - e) *We could hear* [echos / echoes] *but did not know where they were coming from.*
   - f) *She could hear* [women / woman] *chatting in the room next door.*
   - g) *He refused to* [accept / except] *her apology.*
   - h) *She could not* [bear / bare] *the suspense.*
   - i) *That evening, she seemed* [cheerfull / cheerful] *enough.*
   - j) *The protesters did their cause a* [disservice / diservice] *by their violent behaviour.*

TEST YOURSELF

The following tasks will test you on what you have learnt from Part Two.
You can find the answers in Part Seven.

1. Circle the correct spelling.

a) argument / arguement

b) privelige / privilege

c) relevant / relevent

d) protagonist / protaganist

e) accomodation / accommodation

f) liason / liaison

g) separate / seperate

h) parliament / parlament

i) contredict / contradict

j) dissapointed /disappointed

k) mispell / misspell

l) copeing / coping

2. Fill the gaps in these words with the correct letters. The number of letters varies.

a) *These measures are intended to protect the envir..........ment.*

b) *Both vehicles were station..........ry at the time.*

c) *She had had enough of living at home and longed to be independ..........t.*

d) *This speech is the first monolo.......... by the play's protagonist.*

e) *There are several instances of onomatop.......... in the poem.*

f) *She evidently perc..........ves herself to be a great success.*

g) *His father's early death had ....ffected his childhood very profoundly.*

h) *His mood at the end of the scene is upbeat and hopefu.......... .*

3. Write the plural form of these words.

a) woman ....

b) crisis ....

c) phenomenon ....

d) parenthesis ....

e) criterion ....

f) analysis ....

❹ Proofread this student's descriptive essay to find the spelling errors. Circle the errors and write the correct spelling at the side of the page.

My lungs feel as if they are about to burst as I turn into the final straight. With the 25th mile marker passed me, my douts are all behind me. For the first time in this race, I know I am going to make it. Finally, I am going to fullfil my ambition. I force myself to put one blistered and bloodied foot in front of another. Not long to go now – I can do it.

The agony of the last ten miles – a persistant cramp in both calfs – is at last receding and a welcome numness spreads upwards through my legs. Indeed, I can scarcely feel them now. Will they even bare my weight? I look down at them – familar, and yet strangely alien, these appendages that seem to move of their own accord, as if independant of me. The relief, though, is beyond words. In fact, I have no words – no thoughts, even. All I have is focus, one single focus – I must reach that finishing line. Crowds stand at the roadside, cheering and urging us on, but I am scarcely concious of them. I must keep going.

The finish line finally comes into view and I feel a sudden surge of energy and joy – extasy even. This is the moment my hole being has been going towards. I marshal every last ounce of energy and determination to accomplish this one goal. I focus on the finishing line as if my life depends on it and force my body onwards.

PROGRESS CHECK FOR PART TWO

GOOD PROGRESS

I can:

- Apply the main rules and conventions of spelling and spell most common words accurately ☐
- Use at least one mnemonic or other technique to memorise complex spellings ☐

EXCELLENT PROGRESS

I can:

- Apply a wide range of spelling rules and conventions and spell common and more complex words accurately ☐
- Use a range of mnemonics and other techniques to memorise complex spellings ☐

VOCABULARY FOR IMPACT

It is important to understand how to choose vocabulary, both to create maximum impact in your own writing and to analyse literary and persuasive texts. Consider the difference between 'a very big wave' and 'a thundering wall of water', for example. The meaning is essentially the same, but the impact of the second description is far greater, with the word 'thundering' giving a forceful impression of noise, power and danger.

SYNONYMS AND ANTONYMS

Synonyms are words with the same or very similar meaning – for example, 'brave' and 'courageous' or 'wickedness' and 'evil'.

Antonyms are words with opposite meanings. They can be formed with **prefixes** – for example, 'logical' and 'illogical' – or they can be completely different words – for example, 'guilt' and 'innocence'.

Writers use synonyms for the following reasons:

- To avoid repeating words, especially in the same sentence or in adjacent sentences
- To give extra or more precise meaning – for example, using words such as 'mutter', 'squeal', 'cackle' or 'wail' instead of 'say' can help to show the personality or emotions of the person you are writing about
- To add interest and detail to your writing – the examiner will be more impressed by 'the muffled roar of an approaching vehicle' than 'the sound of a car arriving'
- To contribute to the **tone** of a piece – for example, choosing a word such as 'slither' instead of 'move' or 'murky' instead of 'dark' could help to create a frightening atmosphere

TOP TIP 

In creative or descriptive writing, try to avoid very common words such as 'big', 'nice' or 'happy'. Use more interesting or precise synonyms instead.

SHADES OF MEANING

Many words that we think of as synonyms have important shades of meaning. Sometimes they convey a difference in intensity. For example, instead of using the **adjective** 'embarrassing', you might choose 'excruciating' or 'mortifying', which have the same meaning but are more emphatic.

In other cases, synonyms are used to show the opinion of the writer or narrator. Look at these sentences:

*His early life had made him **tough**.*

*His early life had made him **hard**.*

Although 'tough' and 'hard' have similar meanings, the former has positive connotations of being practical and able to deal with life's problems. The latter is more negative, implying a lack of empathy or emotion.

❶ Look at these words. Write 'P' next to positive words, 'N' next to negative words and 'X' next to neutral words.

a) confident [ ]
b) cocky [ ]
c) bumptious [ ]
d) poised [ ]
e) self-possessed [ ]
f) swaggering [ ]

❷ Look at these words. Write 'P' next to positive words, 'N' next to negative words and 'X' next to neutral words.

a) smell [ ]
b) reek [ ]
c) stink [ ]
d) fragrance [ ]
e) aroma [ ]
f) scent [ ]

NOUN PHRASES

A **noun phrase** (sometimes also called an 'expanded noun phrase') is a word or a group of words used as a noun. A noun phrase can be replaced with a **pronoun** such as 'it', 'she' or 'them'.

Noun phrases allow you to add information to a single noun, either before it, after it or on either side of it:

The picture shows ***several modern buildings.***

Buildings made from wood *can be seen in the background.*

The picture is dominated by ***a magnificent marble building decorated with statues.***

Noun phrases are used to avoid short, repetitive sentences and therefore achieve a more elegant, flowing style. Compare these two sentences:

The man was tall. He was standing in the corner. He was Anna's brother.

The tall man standing in the corner *was Anna's brother.*

Noun phrases can be short or long – sometimes very long!

The ocean *appears calm.* (Here, the addition of the **determiner** 'the' makes the noun phrase.)

The turquoise ocean *appears calm.*

The turquoise waters of the ocean, spreading far into the distance, *appear calm.*

CHECK YOUR SKILLS

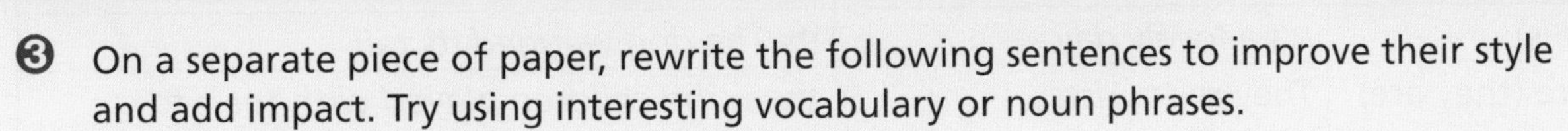

❸ On a separate piece of paper, rewrite the following sentences to improve their style and add impact. Try using interesting vocabulary or noun phrases.

a) *It was raining a lot and our clothes got wet.*
b) *The mountains looked dangerous and were very high.*
c) *The music was soothing. It was beautiful. I let it flow over me.*

WHAT ARE WORD CLASSES?

The term **word class** (sometimes called **part of speech**) refers to a type of word – for example, a noun, verb, **adjective** or **pronoun**. You use these terms when thinking about grammar and the way words behave and link together.

NOUNS

Nouns are words that are used for things, people, places and ideas.

Noun	Definition	Examples
Concrete nouns	Things you can detect with your senses	*water, arm, zebra*
Abstract nouns	Qualities, ideas and concepts	*trust, happiness, protection*
Proper nouns	Names of things such as people, places, historical events, organisations, days and months	*Lady Macbeth, Dunsinane Hill, Battle of Agincourt*

Countable nouns such as 'poet', 'character' or 'simile' can have 'a' or 'an' in front of them, and can be made plural. **Uncountable nouns** (sometimes called mass nouns) such as 'poetry', 'imagery' or 'personification', cannot have 'a' or 'an' in front of them and cannot be made plural.

GET IT RIGHT! 

Use 'less' before uncountable nouns and 'fewer' before countable nouns, e.g. 'less alliteration', 'fewer verses'.

PRONOUNS

Pronouns are words such as 'me', 'theirs', 'this' and 'herself'. They are used to replace nouns or **noun phrases**, usually in order to avoid repetition. Compare these two sentences:

> *Karl works with Anna. Karl sometimes helps Anna because Anna has a lot to do.*
>
> *Karl works with Anna.* ***He*** *sometimes helps* ***her*** *because* ***she*** *has a lot to do.*

When pronouns are followed by short forms of the verb 'be', they often cause problems with spelling because they can be confused with **determiners**. Look at the chart below and learn the correct spellings.

Pronoun	Correct use	Do not confuse with ...
it's (it is)	*It's a lovely day.*	**its** *The dog wagged its tail.*
they're (they are)	*They're tourists.*	**their** *The children played with their toys.* **there** *There's Joe.*
you're (you are)	*You're welcome.*	**your** *Is this your coat?*
who's (who is)	*Who's that man?*	**whose** *Whose pen is this?*

Here are some other issues that can cause difficulties with pronouns:

- **I or me?** This can be difficult when you write about yourself and another person. The simple rule is to use the pronoun you would use if you were only writing about yourself: *Tom and I played tennis*, *Grace invited Tom and me to her party*.
- **Who or whom?** 'Whom' is rarely used in modern English. The only exception is in formal writing when you want to avoid ending a sentence with a **preposition**: *Laurence is the friar from whom Juliet gets the potion* (rather than *The friar who Juliet gets the potion from*).
- **They or he or she/their or his or her?** In modern English, it is usually considered acceptable to use the pronouns 'they' and 'their' to refer to a singular subject in order to avoid the clumsy 'he or she'/'his or her': *Neither Romeo nor Juliet could express their love openly*.

1 Complete these sentences with suitable pronouns.

a) *Is this jacket ....? I found .... lying on the floor.*

b) *Where's Robert? I want to ask .... if he can manage all the work .... or if he needs help.*

c) *Do you know .... book this is? I want to return it to ....*.

VERBS

Verbs are sometimes called 'doing words'. They are used to talk about actions or states. Examples of verbs are 'portray', 'find', 'seem' and 'write'. These examples are in the **root form**, but verbs often change their form according to the **subject** or the **tense** of the verb. For example, the verb 'buy' can take the form 'buys', 'buying' or 'bought'.

TOP TIP

For more information on verb tenses see 'Using tenses consistently' on page 42.

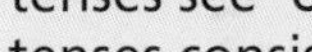

PREPOSITIONS

Prepositions are words such as 'near', 'by', 'under' and 'at'. They tell the reader about the position of things or people, or the relationship between them, for example in these lines from William Wordsworth's poem 'Daffodils':

> ***Beside*** *the lake,* ***beneath*** *the trees,*
> *Fluttering and dancing* ***in*** *the breeze.*

Some verbs, adjectives and nouns must be followed by a particular preposition. For example, 'depend on' (not 'of'), 'similar to' (not 'than') or 'excited about' (not 'for').

GET IT RIGHT!

In modern English, most people accept 'different from' or 'different to'. However, it is safer to stick to 'different from' in formal writing.

ADJECTIVES

Adjectives are words such as 'blue', 'descriptive' and 'figurative'. They are used with nouns and **noun phrases** to add description and detail to writing. Some adjectives can be used to add intensity to descriptions – for example, 'blistering heat', 'crushing defeat'.

You can use **comparative adjectives** to compare things, and **superlative adjectives** to show that something or someone has the most of a particular quality:

Benjamin is ***older*** *than the other animals.*

Some of the animals are ***more intelligent*** *than the others.*

The pigs are the ***cleverest*** *animals.*

The pigs' ***most faithful*** *disciples were the carthorses.*

Adjectives with one **syllable** usually form their comparatives and superlatives by adding '-er' and '-est'. Longer adjectives usually use 'more' and 'most' before the adjective. Two-syllable adjectives can usually use either form. However, there are some common irregular forms:

good → better → best

bad → worse → worst

far → further → furthest

GET IT RIGHT!

Use **either** an '-er' or '-est' form **or** 'more'/'most' for comparative and superlative adjectives. Do not write 'more larger' or 'most heaviest', for example.

When using more than one adjective to describe a single noun, the adjectives usually appear in the order shown in the chart below. Note, however, that it would be very unusual to use more than three adjectives at one time.

Opinion	Size	Shape	Age	Colour	Nationality	Material
important, delicious	*enormous, minuscule*	*square, oval*	*ancient, young*	*turquoise, orange*	*Irish, Russian*	*wooden, furry*

ADVERBS

The term **adverb** covers several types of words that are used to add information to verbs. The main categories are:

- **Manner:** *quietly, reluctantly, fairly*
- **Degree:** *extremely, hardly, very*
- **Frequency:** *sometimes, never, monthly*
- **Time:** *now, tomorrow, soon*
- **Place:** *here, outside, upstairs*

In descriptive writing, adverbs of manner such as 'stealthily', 'greedily' or 'gleefully' can add useful information about the way a character acts. Use them sparingly, however – adding too many can sound clumsy and weaken their impact.

GET IT RIGHT! 

A common error is to use an adjective in places where an adverb should be used:

They were playing their music very loud. ×

They were playing their music very loudly. ✓

❷ Write a suitable adjective or adverb in each gap.

a) *'You're so lucky!' Jan said.............................., staring around at Hugo's .... apartment.*

b) *Having studied so.............................., Philip was .... devastated to fail the exam.*

c) *Her .... hair fell in waves to her waist, gleaming as she moved .... towards us.*

TOP TIP

To learn more about how conjunctions are used to link clauses, see 'Clauses and types of sentences' on page 36.

CONJUNCTIONS

Conjunctions are words that link **clauses** in sentences. There are two types of conjunction:

Conjunction	Used to ...	Examples
Coordinating conjunction	Link two clauses of equal importance	*and, but, or, not, yet, then*
Subordinating conjunction	Link two clauses, one of which develops or adds information to an aspect of the other	*while, although, if, since, because*

DETERMINERS

Determiners are words such as 'a', 'the', 'my', 'each' and 'several'. They are used directly before nouns, and have various functions, such as indicating number, amount and ownership.

CHECK YOUR SKILLS

❸ Look at this excerpt from a student's response to an exam task about role models. Find **seven** errors covered by this unit and write them out correctly on a separate piece of paper.

In my opinion, whether or not celebrities can be true role models depends of why they are famous. A sportsperson or a musician who's skills inspire ordinary people can be a worthy role model, but this is very different than admiring someone merely for there wealth or lifestyle.

However, in general I believe that our society would benefit from choosing role models with more humbler qualities such as kindness and generosity. If less people aspired to wealth and celebrity, I believe we could achieve a more good society for everyone.

CLAUSES AND TYPES OF SENTENCES

It is important to understand the different types of sentence you can use and how they are structured. If you can analyse sentences, you can make sure that you use a variety of them in your writing. You can also ensure that you use the correct punctuation.

PHRASES AND CLAUSES

In grammar, a **phrase** is a single part of a sentence, often consisting of a group of words – for example, 'a blue car' or 'committed a crime'. You use phrases as building blocks to create sentences.

Clauses are often longer. They are short sentences or parts of longer, more complex sentences. Every clause has a subject and a verb:

Subject	Verb	
The actor	starred	in both movies.
We	ate	at a French café.
The plate	broke.	

TYPES OF SENTENCES

Sentences are often grouped into three main types: **simple sentences**, **compound sentences** and **complex sentences**.

A simple sentence consists of one clause, such as the sentences in the chart above.

A compound sentence has two or more clauses that make sense on their own, usually linked with the words 'and, 'or' or 'but':

I eat fish but I don't eat meat.

A complex sentence has two or more clauses. One of the clauses (the **main clause**) makes sense on its own, but the other (the **subordinate clause**) needs the main clause with it in order to make sense. Subordinate clauses start with a word such as 'while', 'if', 'although', 'because' or 'when'. Here are examples of complex sentences:

I like him a lot, although we don't agree on many issues.

I checked my emails while Jamie made coffee.

We need to leave now if we're going to get there on time.

GET IT RIGHT! 

In a complex sentence, if the subordinate clause comes first, a comma is needed after it: *Although he's thin, he's very strong.*

There is an important difference between complex and compound sentences. In a complex sentence, you can usually change the order of the main and subordinate clauses:

I checked my emails while Jamie made coffee. ✓

While Jamie made coffee, I checked my emails. ✓

In a compound sentence, you cannot change the order of the clauses:

I felt tired so I went to bed. ✓

So I went to bed I felt tired. ×

As shown on page 35, the words that link clauses in compound and complex sentences are called **conjunctions**. In a compound sentence, these linking words are called **coordinating conjunctions**. Common coordinating conjunctions are 'and', 'but' and 'or'. In a complex sentence, the linking words are called **subordinating conjunctions**. Examples of subordinating conjunctions are 'if', 'when', 'although', 'because' and 'since'.

MINOR SENTENCES

A **minor sentence** is a short sentence that does not have a main clause. In some contexts, it is not considered to be a proper sentence, but you can use minor sentences for exclamations, sayings or responses to questions. Some examples of minor sentences are:

Happy Birthday.

Hey!

The more the merrier!

CHECK YOUR SKILLS

1. Look at this excerpt from a student's response to a creative writing task. Write the sentence numbers next to the sentence types to identify them. Note that there may be more than one of each type.

> **[1]** The room was dimly lit and I couldn't make out many faces. **[2]** I sat near the door because I wanted Sophie to see me. **[3]** She would arrive soon. **[4]** The sooner, the better. **[5]** The night was young but we had much to discuss.

a) simple sentence [ ]
b) compound sentence [ ]
c) complex sentence [ ]
d) minor sentence [ ]

USING SENTENCES ACCURATELY AND EFFECTIVELY

To use sentences effectively, it is important to consider the sentence types you are using and the impression they convey to the reader. You also need to be aware of common errors with sentences, so that you can be confident about avoiding them.

CHOOSING SENTENCE TYPES FOR STYLE

Most texts work best with a variety of sentence types. This is because a varied text is more likely to hold the reader's interest. In addition, different types of sentence are more suited to particular types of information.

TOP TIP

When revising or doing practice tests, read your work aloud. This will help you check that it flows well and that your choice of sentence types conveys the meaning and style you want.

Simple sentences:

- ✓ Are very clear and easy to understand
- ✓ Can be good for emphasis and impact
- ✓ Can provide a sudden, dramatic shift in **tone** within a more descriptive piece
- × Can sound repetitive and even patronising
- × Can lead to unnecessary repetition of the subject of the sentences

Compound and **complex sentences**:

- ✓ Make your writing flow and often sound more elegant than simple sentences
- ✓ Are good for connecting ideas
- ✓ Can help you avoid repeating the subject of the sentences too often
- × Can be less clear than simple sentences
- × Can lead to important information being 'buried' in a long sentence

Compare the two texts below. Note how the one on the right uses a greater variety of sentence types to create a wider range of effects.

Yosemite National Park is in California. It is named after a tribe that once lived there. It covers an area of over 3,000 square kilometres. Almost four million people go there every year. They want to see the amazing scenery. There are dramatic waterfalls. There are also towering rock faces. Yosemite is also home to giant sequoia trees. The trees grow up to 85 metres tall. They are incredible!

Yosemite National Park is in California. Named after a tribe that once lived there, it covers an area of over 3,000 square kilometres. Almost four million people a year go there to see the amazing scenery, including dramatic waterfalls and towering rock faces. Yosemite is also home to giant sequoia trees, which grow up to 85 metres tall. Incredible!

COMMON ERRORS WITH SENTENCES

In **run-on sentences**, clauses that should form two or more sentences are written together with no punctuation:

Homework often has little value nevertheless most teachers insist on setting it. ×

Homework often has little value. Nevertheless, most teachers insist on setting it. ✓

With a **comma splice**, a comma is written where a full stop or **conjunction** should be used:

I believe that homework is necessary, it consolidates learning done in class. ×

I believe that homework is necessary. It consolidates learning done in class. ✓

I believe that homework is necessary because it consolidates learning done in class. ✓

Remember that a sentence with two main clauses needs a conjunction. If it cannot take a conjunction, such as 'and', 'but' or 'because', you should make it separate sentences or rewrite it with a main and a subordinate clause.

In a **sentence fragment**, a necessary part of the sentence (for example, the subject or the verb) is missing:

So many people on the beach. ×

There were so many people on the beach. ✓

Sentence fragments can sometimes be used for stylistic effect, especially in creative writing. However, unlike minor sentences, they are not part of correct standard English.

In formal written English, you should not start a sentence with a conjunction such as 'and' or 'but':

Karl accepted the decision. But he was still disappointed. ×

Karl accepted the decision but he was still disappointed. ✓

Writers sometimes choose to start sentences with these conjunctions, but only for deliberate stylistic effect.

CHECK YOUR SKILLS

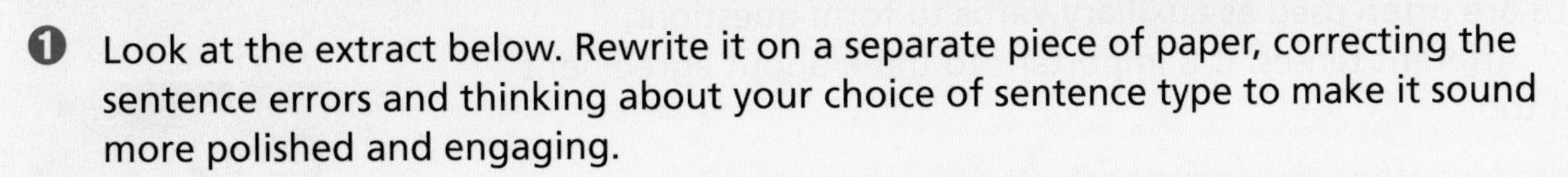

1. Look at the extract below. Rewrite it on a separate piece of paper, correcting the sentence errors and thinking about your choice of sentence type to make it sound more polished and engaging.

I woke up with a start. I looked around. I didn't understand where James had gone. Then I realised what had happened. The jewels and all my money had gone! I can barely describe how I felt at that moment, angry, scared and utterly betrayed. And I had trusted James that was the worst thing, how could I have been so foolish?

SUBJECT AND VERB AGREEMENT

Every sentence has a **subject** and a verb. 'Agreement' means that the form of the verb must match the subject in order to make a grammatically correct sentence.

NUMBER AND PERSON

To get agreement right, you need to think about two things. The first is number – whether the subject is singular or plural. Compare these two sentences:

This character ***appears*** *in Chapter 2.*

These characters ***appear*** *in Chapter 2.*

The second thing to think about is the person – who the subject is. This is important when the subject is a **pronoun**. Compare:

He ***was*** *cold.*

They ***were*** *cold.*

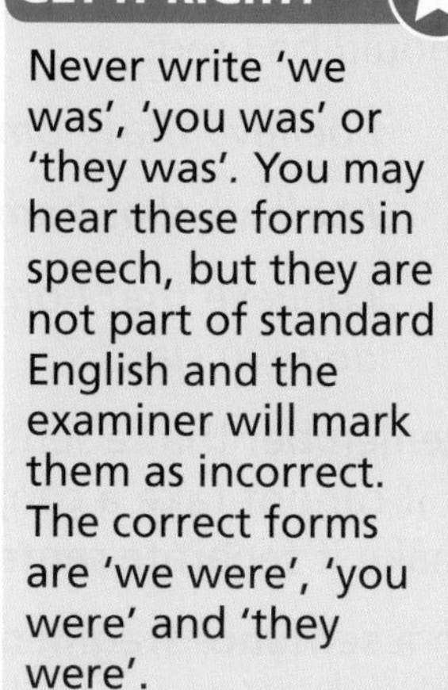

GET IT RIGHT!

Never write 'we was', 'you was' or 'they was'. You may hear these forms in speech, but they are not part of standard English and the examiner will mark them as incorrect. The correct forms are 'we were', 'you were' and 'they were'.

> Remember that if two singular subjects are connected with 'and', the verb agrees as if with a plural subject.

The main house and the cottage ***belong*** *to the squire.*

Sometimes, the subject and verb are a long way apart in a sentence. When that happens, it is especially important to check that they agree, because it is easy to make mistakes:

The scene *in* Animal Farm *in which we first meet the cart-horses Boxer and Clover* ***is*** *…*

IRREGULAR VERBS

Be especially careful with the verbs 'be', 'have' and 'do' because they are irregular:

Mr Jones ***is*** *the owner of the farm.*

Boxer and Clover ***are*** *not very intelligent.*

Irregular verbs are often used as **auxiliary verbs** to form questions, negatives and different tenses. It is important to think about agreement in these cases too:

How ***does*** *the author create sympathy for her characters?*

Do *her friends support her in this scene?*

1 Choose the correct option to complete each sentence.

a) *How* [has / have] *the author used descriptions of colour to indicate mood?*

b) *One of the characters* [is / are] *said to be based on the author's father.*

c) *The poem has six verses, all of similar length, and* [describe / describes] *the changing roles of father and son.*

COMMON ERRORS WITH SUBJECT AND VERB AGREEMENT

The following cases often cause problems for students.

'There is ...' must be followed by a singular subject and 'There are ...' by a plural subject.

*There **is** no description of the mother's physical appearance.*

*There **are** several instances of metaphor in the poem.*

Words such as 'government', 'family' and 'herd', which describe groups of people, animals or things, are known as collective nouns. You can use a singular **or** plural verb with these words, but make sure that you choose one form and use it consistently throughout your piece of writing:

*The Birling family **live/lives** in the fictional town of Brumley.*

Pronouns such as 'everyone' and 'nobody' must agree with a singular verb.

*Anyone who **wants** to do well at school must work hard.*

***Does** everyone have the correct text?*

When 'either' and 'neither' are followed directly by a noun, you should use a singular verb.

*Neither extract **includes** any direct reference to her profession.*

However, when using the phrases 'neither of' or 'either of', you can use a singular or plural verb. Note, however, that it is important to use the same form consistently:

*The narrator does not believe that either of the suspects **is/are** guilty.*

The same is true for 'any of' or 'none of', though the use of a singular verb sounds slightly more formal:

*None of the characters **is/are** portrayed in a sympathetic light.*

CHECK YOUR SKILLS

❷ Correct the errors in these sentences. Tick any sentences that are correct.

a) *In the novel, everyone they encounter try to thwart their efforts.*

b) *She does not believe that any of the servants is trustworthy.*

c) *There is no use of similes in the poem.*

d) *I do not feel that either author succeed in capturing the atmosphere of a fair.*

e) *Everybody in the room have some connection with the dead woman.*

USING TENSES CONSISTENTLY

Tense is the way in which verbs are used to show the time (past, present or future) that the writer is talking about.

PRESENT

The present tense is used for things that are happening now. There are two main forms of present tense in English. The simple present is used for things that happen often or regularly, or that are always true:

*The sun **rises** in the east.*

*Marco **loves** animals.*

The present progressive is used for things that are happening at the time of writing:

*The sun **is rising**.*

Present tenses are frequently used to talk about texts – for example, to describe a plot or to analyse language:

The friar offers Juliet a potion, which she takes the night before her wedding to Paris.

The poet Daljit Nagra uses phrases like 'vee share in di chutney' in order to convey a Punjabi accent in 'Singh Song!'.

When you use the present tense like this, be careful not to change tense in the course of your writing. This is easily done:

*The friar **offers** Juliet a potion, which she **took** the night before her wedding to Paris.* ×

Present tenses can also be a good choice for descriptive or creative writing, because they give a sense of immediacy and draw the reader into the situation:

Darkness falls. Outside, everything is quiet. I can almost hear Dan's heart beating.

FUTURE

Future tenses are used to talk about things that have not happened yet. Unlike many other languages, English does not do this by changing the form of the **root** verb. Instead, there are several ways of talking about the future:

Tense	Used for ...	Example
Present progressive	Things that are decided or arranged	***I'm cooking*** *dinner tonight.*
Present simple	Set times, for example, timetables, opening hours	*The bus **goes** at seven.*
Using 'will'	Offering to do something or when something has just been decided	*I **will cook** dinner tonight.*
With 'going to'	Situations when something has already been decided	*I **am going to cook** dinner tonight.*

PAST

Past tenses are used to talk about things that have already happened.

Tense	Used for ...	Example
Past simple	Events that have a known start and end point	*The three Witches* ***greeted*** *Macbeth.*
Present perfect	Completed events that happen at an unspecified time and which have some relevance to the present	*Lady Macbeth* ***has persuaded*** *her husband to kill Duncan.*
Past perfect	Events that happen before the main story begins	*The Witches* ***had decided*** *to meet with Macbeth.*

All three of these past tense forms also have progressive forms:

They ***were speaking*** *to him.*

They ***have been speaking*** *to him.*

They ***had been speaking*** *to him.*

Progressive forms are often used to talk about something that was happening when something else occurred:

The Birlings ***were having*** *dinner when Inspector Goole* ***arrived****.*

For regular verbs, **past participles** are formed by adding '-ed' to the root word. The perfect tenses also use the **auxiliary verb** 'have':

Gerald ***returned****. / Gerald has* ***returned****. / Gerald had* ***returned****.*

However, many common verbs are irregular:

She ***became*** *a celebrity.*

She has ***become*** *a celebrity.*

GET IT RIGHT! 

Do not use a past participle to form the past simple: 'He ~~come~~ came into the house.'

Do not use the past simple form in a perfect tense: 'She's ~~chose~~ chosen the wrong man to marry.'

CHECK YOUR SKILLS

❶ Complete this chart of irregular past participles.

Root verb	Past simple	Past participle	Root verb	Past simple	Past participle
be	was/were	been	**write**		written
catch	caught		**choose**		chosen
fly		flown	**forgive**	forgave	
hurt	hurt		**throw**		thrown

❷ Complete the sentences with suitable tenses. Use the verbs in brackets. More than one answer may be possible.

a) *Jack's father* .... (come) *back to the house because he* .... (had forgotten) *his umbrella.*

b) *Susie* .... (do) *the cooking yesterday, so I* .... (do) *it today.*

c) *The thieves* .... (break) *into the house while Anna* .... (sleep).

THE POWER OF MODAL VERBS

In English, the **modal verbs** are 'can', 'could', 'may', 'might', 'shall', 'will', 'would', 'must' and 'ought'. Unlike other verbs, they do not add endings such as '-s', '-ing' or '-ed'. They are used with other verbs to express many basic ideas – for example, probability, permission, ability, advice and obligation.

EXPRESSING DEGREES OF CERTAINTY

Modal verbs are often used to say whether something is possible, impossible, probable or certain. Compare the following sentences talking about the future:

*Scientists **will** one day develop robots that are capable of creative thought.*

*Scientists **may/might/could** one day succeed in developing robots that are capable of creative thought.*

Modal verbs are also used to express degrees of certainty about the present or the past:

*Only children **may** have less opportunity to learn how to resolve arguments.*

*Such experiences **must** have had a damaging effect on these children.*

The modal verbs 'could', 'might' and 'would' are useful for presenting opposing viewpoints in an essay:

*Opponents of the idea **would/might** argue that ...*

*It **could** be argued that ...*

When you use modal verbs in the past **tense**, be very careful to form the tenses correctly. It is a common error to use 'of' instead of 'have' because this is what it sounds like in speech. However, this is not correct and you will lose marks for it in an exam:

They suspected that the Inspector could of been a fake. ✗

They suspected that the Inspector could have been a fake. ✓

> **TOP TIP**
>
> Be careful to spell modal verbs correctly. Remember the silent 'l' in 'should', 'could' and 'would'.

PRESENTING ADVICE OR TALKING ABOUT OBLIGATIONS

Modal verbs are also useful for making suggestions or giving opinions about things that should or should not happen:

*Head teachers **could** be more flexible about school uniforms.*

*In my opinion, students **should** not be forced to wear a uniform.*

*All schools **ought to** allow girls to wear trousers.*

NEGATIVES AND SHORT FORMS

The modal verbs 'will' and 'would' are often shortened to *'ll* and *'d,* especially after pronouns such as 'he', 'I' or 'they'.

***They'll** probably ask you to pay.*

*I **don't** know if **he'd** agree to such a proposal.*

However, although they may be used in **dialogue**, these short forms should not be used in formal writing.

Most modal verbs are made negative by adding 'not'. 'Not' is a separate word in all cases except 'cannot'. Remember that the modal verb 'ought' adds 'not' before 'to':

*Schools **ought not to** compel students to wear a uniform.*

In dialogue and informal writing, 'not' is usually shortened to *n't*. Note that some negative modal verbs have slightly irregular forms. Do not use these shortened forms in formal writing.

Modal verb	Negative	Short negative	Modal verb	Negative	Short negative
can	cannot	can't	**could**	could not	couldn't
may	may not	[short form not used in modern English]	**might**	might not	mightn't
must	must not	mustn't	**ought to**	ought not to	oughtn't to
shall	shall not	shan't	**will**	will not	won't
would	would not	wouldn't			

CHECK YOUR SKILLS

1. In these excerpts from a viewpoint essay, 'facts' have been stated with too much certainty and the style is too informal. On a separate piece of paper, rewrite the excerpts in a more appropriate style, using modal verbs where possible. Correct any ungrammatical usages.

   a) The government must ban smoking completely. People who smoke get many serious diseases and our hospitals can't cope with the increasing demands on their services.

   b) The government has already banned smoking in public buildings, but it should of done more. Seeing adults smoke in any situation encourages children to take up the habit.

   c) Smokers will argue that they have a right to smoke but if they insist on that right, they can't expect free health care without paying extra for it.

TEST YOURSELF

Now complete these tasks to check what you have learnt in Part Three. You can find the answers in Part Seven.

1. Sort the words below into four groups of **synonyms**. Add another synonym to each group.

hideous	ideal	serene	unruffled	miserable	flawless
grotesque	wretched	immaculate	placid	heartbroken	ghastly

2. Rewrite the following to make single sentences using **compound sentences, complex sentences** or **noun phrases.**

   a) *We saw a castle. It was on top of a hill. It was ruined.*

   ....

   b) *Rob loved swimming. He had to get up very early to practise though.*

   ....

   c) *One girl distracted the man. The other girl stole his passport.*

   ....

   d) *There was a crowd. It was huge. The people in it were tourists.*

   ....

   e) *Maria plays the piano. Charlie also plays the piano. Rory doesn't.*

   ....

3. Look at the words in the box. Sort them into their correct **word classes** in a table like the one below.

year	at	remember	Marilyn	extremely	bold	and	or	my
reckon	those	from	heavily	me	mine	glamorous		

Noun	Pronoun	Verb	Adjective	Adverb	Preposition	Conjunction	Determiner

4. Look at these sentences. Tick the sentences that are grammatically correct, and correct the ones that are not.

   a) *We cannot be sure whether either character are telling the truth.*

   b) *Meena steals sweets from a shop but was caught by her father.*

   c) *None of the children remember their father.*

   d) *Macbeth is reassured by the witches' prophecies because he knows that trees cannot move.*

   e) *He is happy because Anna has forgave him.*

⑤ Find and correct **eight** mistakes in this excerpt from a student's article giving advice to young people about coping with stress.

Sometimes its easy to feel that everyone expects us to be perfect. We think that if only we was prettier, cleverer or more popular, life would be more easier and we would have less problems. It's not surprising if these high expectations causes stress.

The first thing to say is don't worry stress is a normal part of life, but if your feeling really bad, the worse thing you can do is bottle up your feelings, so find someone to talk to.

⑥ On a separate piece of paper, rewrite this introductory paragraph from a narrative story. Improve the style and impact by choosing a wider range of vocabulary and sentence types.

Mrs Hobson was our neighbour. She was very old. My parents used to say that Mrs Hobson was eccentric. They told me she'd been a singer. I was scared of Mrs Hobson. I thought she looked like a witch. She was thin. She had arthritis in her fingers and her skin had lots of wrinkles. She had an unpleasant voice. She cooked stews that smelt horrible. What I did to her was wrong though. There was no excuse for it.

PROGRESS CHECK FOR PART THREE

GOOD PROGRESS

I can:

- Use varied and appropriate vocabulary to give impact to my writing ☐
- Use language concepts such as sentence structure, word class, subject-verb agreement and tense to write well-formed text ☐
- Use my knowledge of these issues to analyse texts and describe the language an author uses ☐

EXCELLENT PROGRESS

I can:

- Use a wide range of vocabulary and choose words with appropriate shades of meaning in order to give my writing impact and nuance ☐
- Vary the pace and tone of my writing by using different types of sentence structure ☐
- Write well-formed, grammatically correct text with accuracy and confidence ☐
- Analyse and describe the language in a text and make a well-reasoned assessment of why an author has chosen particular language features ☐

FULL STOPS, QUESTION MARKS AND EXCLAMATION MARKS

It is important to use punctuation accurately, because it provides structure to your writing and helps the reader navigate texts. Punctuation can also be used to achieve particular stylistic effects.

FULL STOPS

Full stops are used to end sentences.

Meena's friend is called Anita.

Make sure you use a full stop every time it is needed. It is a common error to run two sentences together into a single sentence, or to use a comma where a full stop is needed:

Meena's cousins visit. They are good Indian girls. ✓

Meena's cousins visit they are good Indian girls. ×

Meena's cousins visit, they are good Indian girls. ×

Full stops were often used in the past for abbreviations and short forms of words – for example, *U.S.A., Ltd., St.*. However, conventions are changing and it is now more common to omit full stops in these cases.

It is also unnecessary, though not wrong, to add full stops to titles – for example, *Dr Smith, Ms Lamb*. It is more common to use full stops when the short form of a word does not include its last letter – for example, *Capt.* (Captain), *Co.* (Company), *No.* (Number).

Some authors are known by their initials and family name. In these cases, it is usual to add full stops to the initials: *J. B. Priestley, J. K. Rowling, F. Scott Fitzgerald, A. S. Byatt.*

Some common Latin abbreviations are used in modern English. These are usually written with full stops, as shown in the chart below.

The author J. K. Rowling

Abbreviation	Short for	Meaning	Example
a.m.	*ante meridiem*	before midday	*We got up at five a.m.*
e.g.	*exempli gratia*	for example	*Use an interesting adjective, e.g. 'luminous'.*
etc.	*et cetera*	and others (used to refer to other, similar things)	*She has a great interest in art, music, poetry, etc.*
i.e.	*id est*	that is (used to explain something in other words)	*She was there all winter, i.e. from November to January.*
p.m.	*post meridiem*	after midday	*The train leaves at 6 p.m.*

QUESTION MARKS

As the name implies, question marks are used at the end of a question.

How do the two texts differ in style?

Note that some questions, especially in speech, are phrased like statements. However, they still need a question mark:

'You've never met him before?' she asked.

Rhetorical questions are often used as a stylistic device in texts. In creative writing, they may be used to express emotions such as surprise or anxiety:

Ben knew he must tell the truth. But how would his father react?

They are also used in factual or persuasive writing as a way of emphasising a point or indicating that information or recommendations will follow:

How can we reduce waste? First, try to avoid products with excessive amounts of packaging.

Be careful not to use question marks when you report a question that someone else has asked:

She asked me if I knew where the station was.

EXCLAMATION MARKS

Exclamation marks are used to indicate shock, surprise or urgency.

The room was empty!

'Quick! Climb out of the window!' said Philip.

Exclamation marks are not usually suitable in a formal piece of writing such as an essay about a set novel or play.

TOP TIP

Use exclamation marks sparingly. As a general rule, do not use more than two or three in a single piece of writing, otherwise their effect is weakened.

CHECK YOUR SKILLS

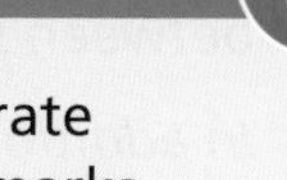

1. Read this excerpt from a student's piece of creative writing. Copy it out on a separate piece of paper, adding capital letters, full stops, question marks and exclamation marks to punctuate it correctly.

I was on holiday in France with my family Mum and Dad were sunbathing on the beach my brother and I were playing at the water's edge, letting the waves knock us over suddenly, I saw a giant wave coming towards us it was as high as a house it crashed over us and I could feel myself being sucked underneath was this it was I going to die

COMMAS

Commas are used between clauses in a sentence or to separate items in lists. When you read aloud, a comma indicates a small pause. This often helps to make the structure and meaning of a sentence clearer.

SEPARATING CLAUSES AND ADDING EXTRA INFORMATION

Commas are often used between a **subordinate clause** and a **main clause**, especially if the subordinate clause comes first:

Although the events in the novel are fictional, they are intended as a warning to modern society.

They are not usually used between main clauses, except when the subject of each clause is different:

Eric has a drinking problem, but his family try to ignore it.

Commas are also used to separate parts of sentences known as **relative clauses**, which give extra information about something or someone:

Stevenson's novella, which was first published in 1886, shows the influence of Charles Darwin's work.

Eric, who has a drinking problem, also knew the dead woman.

GET IT RIGHT!

Do not use a comma between two separate sentences. Use a full stop or link the sentences with a **conjunction**.

ADVERBS AND ADVERBIAL PHRASES

It is very common in essay writing to use **adverbs** such as 'however', 'nevertheless' and 'firstly', or **adverbial phrases** such as 'despite this' or 'in addition' to link and contrast ideas. When these words or phrases come at the beginning of a sentence, they should be followed by a comma:

Moreover, I believe that uniforms promote a sense of equality between school pupils.

In addition, smoking can have a harmful effect on non-smokers.

❶ Add commas where they are needed in the following sentences.

a) *Dr Jekyll who wants to suppress his evil impulses creates a potion to help him do this.*

b) *Moreover homework which can take up a lot of a pupil's time has not been proved to be beneficial.*

c) *However uniforms can enforce a sense of discipline in school.*

LISTS

Commas are used to separate items in a list of three or more people or things:

The poet often compares people to animals such as lions, horses, bears or oxen.

The words 'and' or 'or' are often written before the last item in a list. Some people put a comma before these words and some do not. Either way is correct, but be consistent with the method you choose. One reason to include a final comma is to avoid ambiguity. For example, in the following sentence, it is not clear whether 'economics' and 'politics' are separate courses or one combined course:

Courses offered include: history, art and literature, geography, economics and politics.

Commas are also used between two or more **adjectives**, but only if you can put the word 'and' between the adjectives, and if you can change their order. Compare the following:

We walked down a steep, winding path.

We walked down some steep stone stairs.

In the second sentence, you would not say 'stone steep stairs', so no comma is needed.

TOP TIP 

You are unlikely to use question tags or names in formal essays, but they are important for **dialogue** in creative writing.

OTHER USES OF COMMAS

Commas are also used before question tags such as 'isn't it?' or 'haven't they?' and before names or phrases used in the same way as names:

You don't have a pen I could borrow, do you?

I'm so angry, James.

CHECK YOUR SKILLS

❷ Read this excerpt from a student's piece of descriptive writing. Copy it out on a separate piece of paper, adding commas where necessary.

Although it was midday a strange silence had descended. The street below my apartment usually so bustling and cheerful was deserted. I peered anxiously out of the window unable to make sense of my surroundings. The whole city seemed to be permeated with a ghostly yellowish light.

Cars were still and abandoned shops had their shutters down and even the dogs had stopped their barking.

I went into my room and took out a suitcase. Clothes toothbrush passport. I knew I had to get away.

BRACKETS AND DASHES

Brackets and dashes are used for several reasons. The most common reason is to add extra information, in a similar way to when you might say 'Oh, by the way …' in speech.

BRACKETS

Round brackets are used to give extra information about something or someone.

My sister (who was only seven at the time) was extremely excited.

They can also be used to give alternatives:

The student(s) will receive a prize.

All members (or their representatives) may speak for a maximum of five minutes.

GET IT RIGHT! 

Using round brackets to add information gives writing a slightly informal style. In a more formal essay, use commas instead.

Square brackets are used mainly in very formal, academic writing. Their main use is in quotations, to add explanations or to replace words used in the original in order to make the meaning clear.

Stella insisted that [her parents] had not known of her plan. (Here, 'her parents' replaces 'they'.)

Square brackets can also contain three dots (called an ellipsis, plural **ellipses**) to show that some words have been omitted:

One critic described the novel as 'Harrowing […] and extremely difficult to read.'

When you use brackets, it is important to get the punctuation of the sentence correct. Words inside the brackets should start with a lower-case letter, unless the first word is a **proper noun**. Punctuation should come **outside** the brackets, as if the bracketed information were not present:

Although I met her regularly (at least once a month), we did not become friends.

The only time punctuation should be used inside the brackets is when it applies only to the bracketed words and not to the rest of the sentence:

Martha had nine (nine!) sisters.

1 Correct the errors in these sentences.

a) *Make sure you bring walking boots, a drink (In a flask), a map and binoculars.*

b) *We tried a variety of activities (climbing abseiling and archery), on the course.*

c) *He received a letter from [The boy's father.]*

DASHES

Dashes are used to add extra information. They are less informal than brackets and may be particularly appropriate in creative or descriptive writing. When dashes are used like this, they have a space on either side.

The wet grass – shining in the moonlight – brushed against our bare legs.

Dashes are also used without spaces. They can indicate a range:

More information about metaphor can be found on pages 23–25.

They can also be used between the names of destinations – for example on a train route:

the London–Manchester train

HYPHENS

The most common use of hyphens is to split words at the end of a line in order to make them fit the page. Make sure you split words at an appropriate place, usually between **syllables** or between two words in a compound word such as 'wheelbarrow' or 'suitcase'.

There should be no spaces around a hyphen.

Hyphens are also used in the following situations:

- In multi-word **adjectives** that come before a noun: 'a well-known author', 'an up-to-date system'
- After **prefixes** if the second word begins with a capital letter or if the resulting word looks clearer with a hyphen than without: 'pro-European', 're-examine'
- In some compound words, such as 'bird-watching' or 'wide-ranging'. Unfortunately, there is no clear rule for this – check a dictionary if possible, or think about whether the word is clearer with or without a hyphen

GET IT RIGHT!

Multi-word adjectives that come **after** a noun should **not** be hyphenated: *The author is well known. This information is completely up to date.*

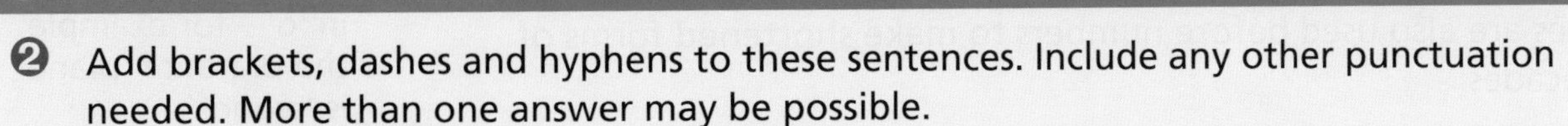

CHECK YOUR SKILLS

❷ Add brackets, dashes and hyphens to these sentences. Include any other punctuation needed. More than one answer may be possible.

a) *If students experience physical symptoms of stress racing heartbeat dizziness etc. they should see the college nurse.*

b) *Hastie Lanyon once a close friend of Jekyll is a very respectable doctor.*

c) *Children in the 3–6 age group may not yet have learnt sufficient self control.*

APOSTROPHES

Apostrophes are used for two main reasons: to show possession in phrases ('Orwell's novel') and to represent missing letters in contracted words ('don't', 'I've'). It is important to take care with apostrophes, as they are the source of many errors.

POSSESSION

This chart shows the rules for using apostrophes for possession.

When to use	Rule	Example
Singular word not ending in 's'	Use *'s*	*the poet's life, a lion's roar*
Singular words ending in 's'	Use either *'s* or *'*, but be consistent; it is becoming more common to use *'s*, especially when the word is pronounced with the sound *iz* at the end	*James's sister, the rhinoceros' horn*
Two singular words	Use *'s* after the second word only	*Anita and Meena's friendship*
Plural word ending in 's'	Use *'*	*the characters' names, the animals' living conditions*
Plural words not ending in 's'	use *'s*	*the women's names*

Although you can use apostrophes to show possession with objects ('the verse's length'), it is much more common to use a phrase with 'of' ('the length of the verse').

With the phrase 'each other', use *'s*:

They even wore each other's clothes.

Apostrophes are also used before numbers to make shortened forms of years or decades:

they met in '95

music of the '60s.

Never use an apostrophe to form a plural. Be especially careful with words ending in 'o' – for example, the plural of 'piano' is 'pianos'.

1 Add apostrophes where they are needed in these sentences.

a) *Meena and her friend take the Rutters poodle to Dale End Farm.*

b) *Anita and Meena go to each others houses.*

c) *Anita and Meena are chased by dogs, and Meena loses her mothers diamond necklace.*

d) *Sam and Anitas taunting messages distract Meena from her revision.*

CONTRACTIONS

Apostrophes are used to make short forms of words. They show that letters are missing.

You should not use **contractions** in formal writing, but you can use them in informal writing or when writing speech.

Contractions are often used for the verbs 'be' and 'have':

be	have
I'm = am	I've, you've, we've, they've = have
he's, she's, it's, who's, there's = is	he's, she's, it's, who's, there's = has
you're, we're, they're = are	I'd, you'd, he'd, she'd, it'd, we'd, they'd, who'd = had

Note that *'s* can represent both 'is' and 'has':

Laura's very tall.

Laura's got two brothers.

The contraction *'ve* is sometimes added to **modal verbs** when representing speech:

'I should've called first,' he said.

The contraction *n't* (a short form of 'not') is often used to make negative forms of the **auxiliary verbs** 'is', 'have' and 'do' and modal verbs:

The man wasn't listening.

We haven't been to the exhibition.

Don't you want to meet her?

You shouldn't write on the question paper.

The modal verbs 'would' and 'will' are often contracted to *'d* and *'ll* when they are followed by another verb, particularly in speech:

I'd like to speak to the manager.

Tom'll meet us later.

It is possible to combine two contractions where this is a representation of the way someone speaks:

'I'd've preferred water,' he complained.

CHECK YOUR SKILLS

❷ Rewrite these sentences on a separate sheet of paper, using contractions where possible.

a) *I am late for school, so it would be great if you would give me a lift.*

b) *We did not see Ed because he had already left before we arrived.*

c) *I do not know who is coming to the meeting we have organised.*

d) *We will go for a walk later if the weather is good.*

COLONS AND SEMICOLONS

Colons and **semicolons** are used to separate parts of sentences. They are often used for reasons of style. They indicate a slightly more definite break than a comma, but a slightly less definite one than a full stop.

COLONS BETWEEN CLAUSES

Colons can be used between two **main clauses** when the second clause gives more information about or more explanation of the first. The first word after the colon should begin with a lower-case letter unless it is a **proper noun**:

Heaney's poem describes the shift in relationship between him and his father: his father, once strong, is now the vulnerable one.

The tone is very informal: casual phrases contrast with the horror of what is being described.

In cases like this, a full stop could be used instead, but the colon shows that there is a strong connection between the two clauses.

Colons are also used between clauses (not necessarily both main clauses) to indicate that something specific is going to be stated or asked:

Nobody has asked the most important question: do children gain anything from this rule?

The poet chooses this adjective for a reason: to give a sense of strangeness to the description of the scene.

In the examples above, the sentences are part of a block of running text. However – as you will see many times in this book – colons can be used before an example that follows on the line below. In this case, it is usual to indent the example.

> **GET IT RIGHT!**
> You should not use a colon after 'e.g.' or directly after a phrase like 'such as'.

COLONS FOR LISTS AND HEADINGS

Another common use of the colon is to introduce a list:

There are four main characters: Dr Jekyll, Mr Hyde, Gabriel Utterson, and Hastie Lanyon.

Colons are also used after short, introductory headings – for example, on a timetable or as part of a set of instructions:

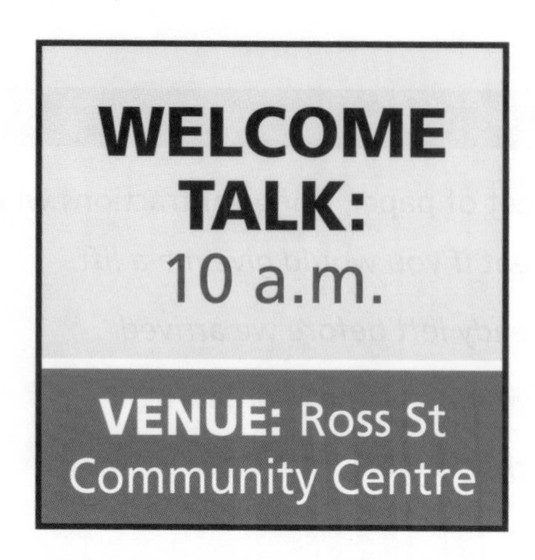

WELCOME
TALK:
10 a.m.
VENUE: Ross St
Community Centre

SEMICOLONS

Semicolons are used between two main clauses. They could be replaced by a full stop or a **conjunction** such as 'and', but their use emphasises the connection between the clauses. There is no watertight rule about when to use a semicolon rather than a colon. However, there are some guidelines you can follow, which are explained below.

Unlike colons, semicolons can **only** be used between main clauses, not between main and **subordinate clauses**:

There was one thing we particularly loved: magic shows. ✓

There was one thing we particularly loved; magic shows. ×

Magic shows were great; we loved them more than anything else. ✓

Semicolons rather than colons are generally used where there is a comparison or contrast between two clauses:

The animals begin to argue more. Snowball wants to build a windmill to generate electricity; Napoleon opposes the plan.

When they are used to divide clauses in this way, both colons and semicolons should be used sparingly – perhaps once or twice per essay.

Semicolons can also be used (instead of commas) to divide items in lists if the items themselves are phrases or clauses. This removes ambiguity about where an item begins and ends, particularly if the items themselves contain commas:

Prizes were awarded as follows: maths, Elise Goodwin; creative writing, Oscar Fisher; photography, Raj Gohil.

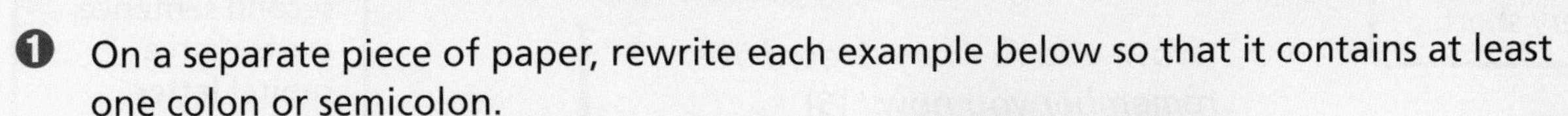

CHECK YOUR SKILLS

1. On a separate piece of paper, rewrite each example below so that it contains at least one colon or semicolon.

   a) *Meena's parents are from a region on the India–Pakistan border. In India, Hindus were in the majority. In Pakistan, most of the population was Muslim.*

   b) *Shelley's poem 'Ozymandias' is about the ephemeral nature of power. The ruined statue contrasts starkly with its arrogant inscription.*

   c) *In the town, it was a morning like any other. Harassed commuters rushed from the station. In the market, traders were setting up their stalls. Tourists paused a moment to take in the scene.*

EFFECTIVE SPEECH PUNCTUATION

If you read a large number of novels, you will see speech punctuated in a variety of ways. However, when you write speech in an exam, you should stick to the conventional rules described here, paying particular attention to the position of punctuation marks.

DIRECT SPEECH

Inverted commas (also called **quotation marks** or, more informally, speech marks) should always be used for direct speech, i.e. around actual spoken words. They can be written as ' ' or " ". Single inverted commas are more common for British English, but whichever you choose, be consistent throughout your piece of writing.

Here are the basic rules:

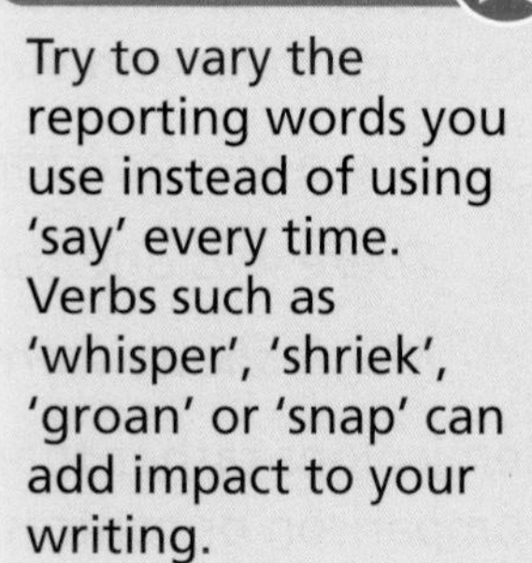

TOP TIP

Try to vary the reporting words you use instead of using 'say' every time. Verbs such as 'whisper', 'shriek', 'groan' or 'snap' can add impact to your writing.

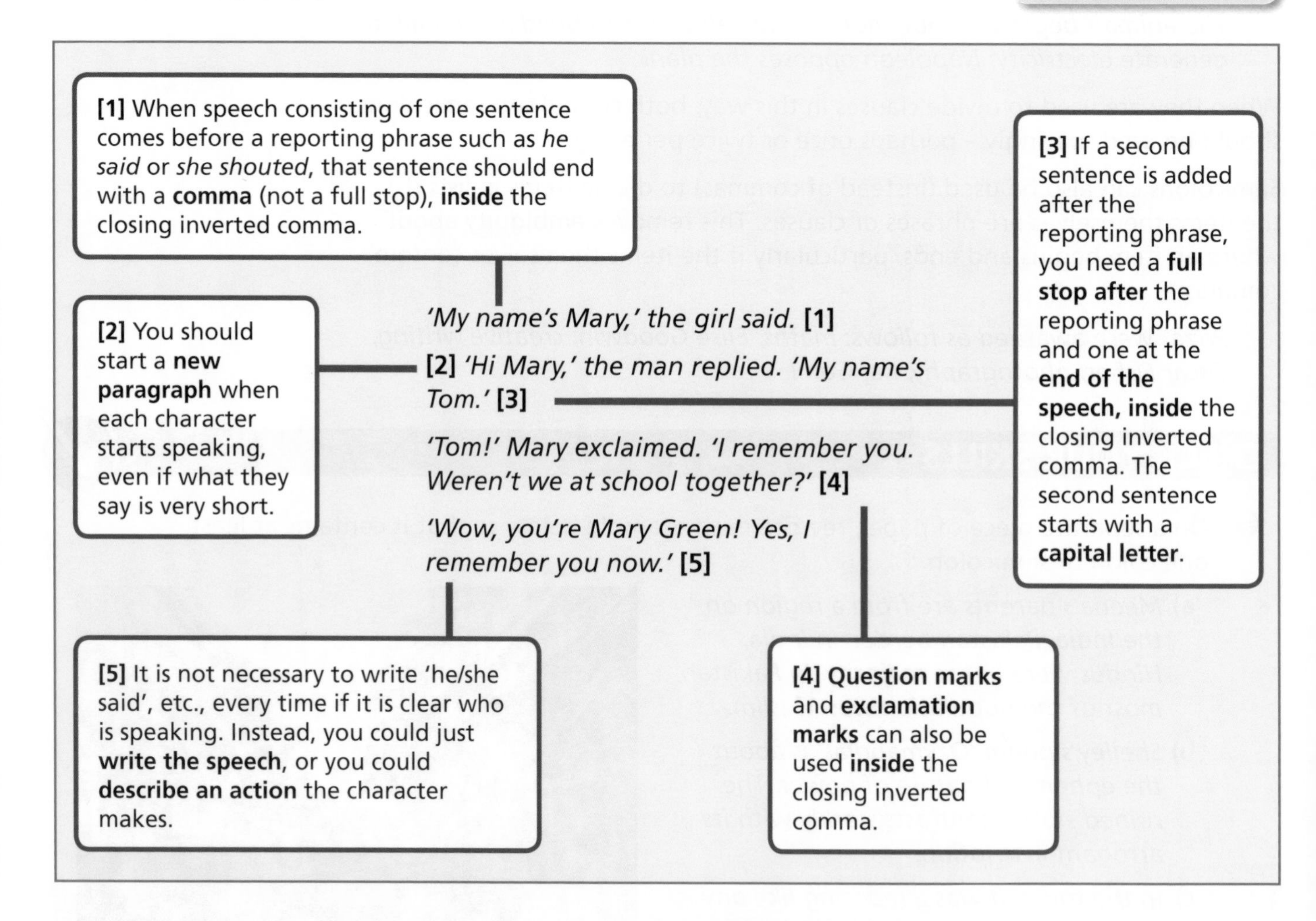

[1] When speech consisting of one sentence comes before a reporting phrase such as *he said* or *she shouted*, that sentence should end with a **comma** (not a full stop), **inside** the closing inverted comma.
[2] You should start a **new paragraph** when each character starts speaking, even if what they say is very short.
'My name's Mary,' the girl said. **[1]**
[2] *'Hi Mary,' the man replied. 'My name's Tom.'* **[3]**
'Tom!' Mary exclaimed. 'I remember you. Weren't we at school together?' **[4]**
'Wow, you're Mary Green! Yes, I remember you now.' **[5]**
[3] If a second sentence is added after the reporting phrase, you need a **full stop after** the reporting phrase and one at the **end of the speech, inside** the closing inverted comma. The second sentence starts with a **capital letter**.
[5] It is not necessary to write 'he/she said', etc., every time if it is clear who is speaking. Instead, you could just **write the speech**, or you could **describe an action** the character makes.
[4] Question marks and **exclamation marks** can also be used **inside** the closing inverted comma.

When speech comes after a reporting phrase, you need a comma **before** the opening inverted comma, and a full stop at the end of the speech, inside the closing inverted comma:

> *Mary said, 'I live next door.'*

It is possible to split a single sentence of speech with a reporting phrase. In this case, use a comma after the first part, a comma after the reporting phrase, and a lower-case letter at the beginning of the second part:

> *'I'm extremely disappointed,' Max said, 'not to have heard from you earlier.*

QUOTATIONS

Inverted commas are used to quote directly from written sources:

The Friar warns them that 'violent delights have violent ends'.

Owen's descriptions of the weather, for example 'merciless iced east winds' and 'the air that shudders black with snow', add to the sense of misery in this poem.

No other punctuation is needed unless the quotation itself includes it.

INDIRECT SPEECH

Inverted commas are **not** used for **indirect speech**:

Papa says that Meena should sing her own songs.

❶ Correct the punctuation errors in these sentences.

a) *'Let me help you,' she offered, 'It's too much work for you to do alone'.*

b) *'I have never', Catherine declared, 'Seen anything like this before.'*

c) *The young man told us 'that he was lost'.*

d) *Kira asked 'Who is in charge here'?*

CHECK YOUR SKILLS

❷ On a separate piece of paper, rewrite the following as speech in a piece of creative writing. Use your own ideas for reporting phrases.

Ben: *This is it! This is the cave I was telling you about.*

Freddy: *Wow! How did you find it?*

Ben: *Do you remember the old book I found in the log cabin?*

Freddy: *The one the old man wrote?*

Ben: *Yes. It had a map in it, and instructions about how to get down to the shore.*

TEST YOURSELF

Now complete these tasks to check what you have learnt in Part Four.
You can find the answers in Part Seven.

1 Add an exclamation mark or a question mark to each of these sentences. You will sometimes need to replace existing punctuation.

a) *'It's unfair, isn't it,' Sophie complained. 'Mum won't let us go with her.'*

b) *He cycled over 200 (that's two hundred) miles a day.*

c) *'Arnie's never had a pizza' Joel exclaimed.*

d) *Can this trend be reversed. Experts say that it can, but only with difficulty.*

2 These sentences use commas incorrectly. Correct each sentence in a different way, using a different punctuation mark or a **conjunction**. There is more than one possible answer for each one.

a) *Harri's relationship with the English language is complex, English is the official language of Ghana but many words are still unfamiliar.*

b) *Daniel was confident, his brother was very shy.*

c) *The texts are very different. The first author uses a lot of description, the second author has a much plainer style.*

3 Add **brackets** or **dashes** to these sentences.

a) *Macbeth wonders if the witches' prophecy that he will become king could be true.*

b) *Kelman suggests that children whether native or immigrant had terrible lives in Britain.*

c) *The excursion paid for by Laurie's father was a great success.*

4 Correct the punctuation errors in these sentences. Tick any sentences that are correct.

a) *Heaney uses the adjective wizened to describe the earth.*

b) *Meena resents the Aunties' interference in her life.*

c) *'You'll need this', Dexter said.*

d) *The man asked us where we were from?*

e) *'You're right,' Carrie agreed. 'We need help.'*

5 Proofread this excerpt from a piece of creative writing. Copy it out on a separate piece of paper, correcting the errors.

> I woke up with a start there was a hammering noise coming from the other side of the wall.
>
> 'Wake up Hettie!' I hissed at my sister, 'Theres someone in Dad's study'. 'Oh no!' she said, climbing out of bed.
>
> We walked across the cold bare floorboards and out onto the landing. Everything was quiet even the wind had stopped it's howling.

Hettie who is never usually scared, looked pale.

'Ive just remembered', she whispered, 'What that man on the horse told us. He was right wasn't he?'

I froze. Could it really be true! Could the thing we'd been dreading for so long really be happening?

6 Copy this paragraph from a student's opinion essay, adding any missing punctuation.

In conclusion I feel that the advantages of TV outweigh the disadvantages. Although many children watch too much TV this is really their parents responsibility not that of the TV companies. Many childrens programmes are educational and adults can learn from TV too with documentaries news programmes and even dramas which introduce them to new concepts. Moreover TV is not only about education relaxation and entertainment are important elements of an enjoyable life too.

PROGRESS CHECK FOR PART FOUR

GOOD PROGRESS

I can:

- Use the most important forms of punctuation accurately ❑
- Make appropriate punctuation choices based on the formality or informality of my text ❑
- Usually understand the function of punctuation in the written works of other authors ❑

EXCELLENT PROGRESS

I can:

- Use a wide range of punctuation accurately ❑
- Make considered punctuation choices in order to achieve a particular stylistic effect ❑
- Understand and am able to analyse the function or stylistic effect of punctuation in the written works of other authors ❑

USING PARAGRAPHS EFFECTIVELY

A paragraph is a section of text that starts on a new line, usually indented a little way, and which contains at least one sentence. Typically, a paragraph deals with a single **theme** or idea. Paragraphs are helpful for the reader, as they break up text into smaller, more manageable units. Paragraphs also help the reader to follow the thread of a story or argument by signalling when a new idea or topic is being introduced.

USING PARAGRAPHS IN CREATIVE WRITING

Writers use paragraphs in several ways in stories. For example, a new paragraph is generally used to introduce a character that is new to the story:

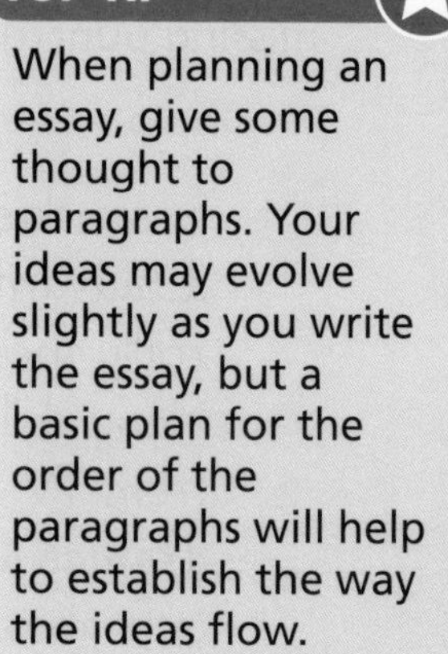

TOP TIP
When planning an essay, give some thought to paragraphs. Your ideas may evolve slightly as you write the essay, but a basic plan for the order of the paragraphs will help to establish the way the ideas flow.

> *Edward placed his book on the bedside table and his glasses neatly beside it, then closed his eyes.*
>
> *Three houses further down the street,* ***a young woman*** *was looking at herself in the mirror. She was dark-haired, with a pale, almost sickly complexion.*

A new paragraph is also used to describe the thoughts or actions of a different character:

> *... Lara gathered her bags and walked smartly out of the room, shutting the door behind her.*
>
> ***James looked up briefly,*** *then resumed his reading. She would be back, of that he was certain.*

A writer may start a new paragraph to introduce a different idea:

> *She hid the paper under her bed. She would read it tomorrow when Al was at work.*
>
> *At least* ***the house was quiet now*** *and she could hear herself think.*

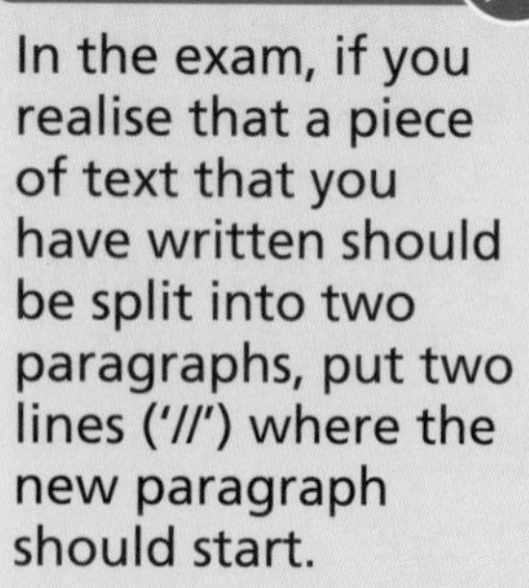

GET IT RIGHT!
In the exam, if you realise that a piece of text that you have written should be split into two paragraphs, put two lines ('//') where the new paragraph should start.

A new paragraph is also used when the action described is happening at a different time:

> *It was getting late and Lara's head was starting to ache again. She began to wish that David hadn't left.*
>
> ***Later that evening,*** *in the apartment below, Mrs Walker was speaking to her son.*

Finally, a new paragraph is used to change speakers in a **dialogue**:

> *Later that evening, Rachel told him about Bethan's comment. He was astonished.*
>
> *'What, in front of your mum and dad?'*
>
> *'Yes, to their faces. Can you believe it?' Rachel asked.*
>
> *'No! What was she thinking? She must be out of her mind!'*

GET IT RIGHT! 

Never combine the speech of two or more characters in one paragraph, as this is likely to confuse the reader.

1 Indicate with two lines ('//') where you would start new paragraphs in this long block of text.

> Claudia hadn't really looked at him properly before. She'd acquired a general impression of him, but that was all. Now, in the bright winter light, she regarded him and took in the details – the set of his square jaw, the sprinkling of grey hairs at the temple. He was what most people would describe as handsome. 'So when are you leaving?' he enquired. 'Next week.' she replied. 'It's suddenly so close! I still have so much packing to do.' 'Well, good luck with it all.' 'Yes, thanks!' His eye was suddenly drawn to the young man behind her, who he then hailed with a friendly 'Hey!'. Their conversation was over. That evening, as she surveyed the untidy mound of unpacked boxes, she reflected on her brief conversation with her soon-to-be ex-neighbour. Why had she felt so awkward? Why hadn't she been able to think of anything amusing or interesting to say? What a missed opportunity!

USING PARAGRAPHS IN PERSUASIVE WRITING

Persuasive essays – for example, in English Language and Literature – typically require three types of paragraph: an introductory paragraph, several 'body' paragraphs and a concluding paragraph.

- The introductory paragraph should convey the subject of the essay but also give some indication of the writer's opinion.
- The 'body' paragraphs convey the main points of the essay. Each new paragraph should make a new point.
- The concluding paragraph restates the main points of the argument and, where possible, gives a summarising statement.

In the main body of the essay (i.e. the middle part), paragraphs should be used to make different points, with each paragraph conveying a new point or focus:

Note that the paragraphs are all indented.

Save the panda, save the world

This paragraph explains the point of view that too much money is spent on panda conservation. Note that it is also possible to present two opposing viewpoints in one paragraph.

Some people argue that the considerable sums of money spent on panda conservation are excessive and not worthwhile. Admittedly, pandas are extraordinarily expensive to protect. Our money, they claim, would be better spent on preserving complex ecosystems such as rainforests, thereby conserving countless other endangered species.

This puts forward an opposing argument and is therefore a new paragraph.

However, this argument overlooks the fact that pandas are in and of themselves a precious species that is worthy of conserving. Are we really prepared to accept a world without these iconic creatures? After all, something about this animal's appearance and behaviour is irresistibly appealing to people, both young and old. Our lives would be impoverished by their disappearance.

This paragraph now adds a supporting point in order to develop the argument in the second paragraph.

Furthermore, the very fact that this species of bear attracts so much attention raises consciousness of the growing phenomenon of animal extinction. It may be regrettable that we care less about the disappearance of unattractive reptiles and insects, but it is a fact. The plight of the cute and charismatic panda draws attention to the dwindling numbers of less photogenic creatures and in that way raises awareness of the problem more generally.

TOPIC SENTENCES

A **topic sentence** is a sentence that gives the reader the main idea of the paragraph. It is often (but not always) the first sentence in a paragraph. The topic sentence relates to the overall theme of the essay, but focuses on a specific aspect of it, which can then be developed within the paragraph. The sentences that follow the topic sentence should all relate to it, providing facts or points that are relevant or prove it in some way.

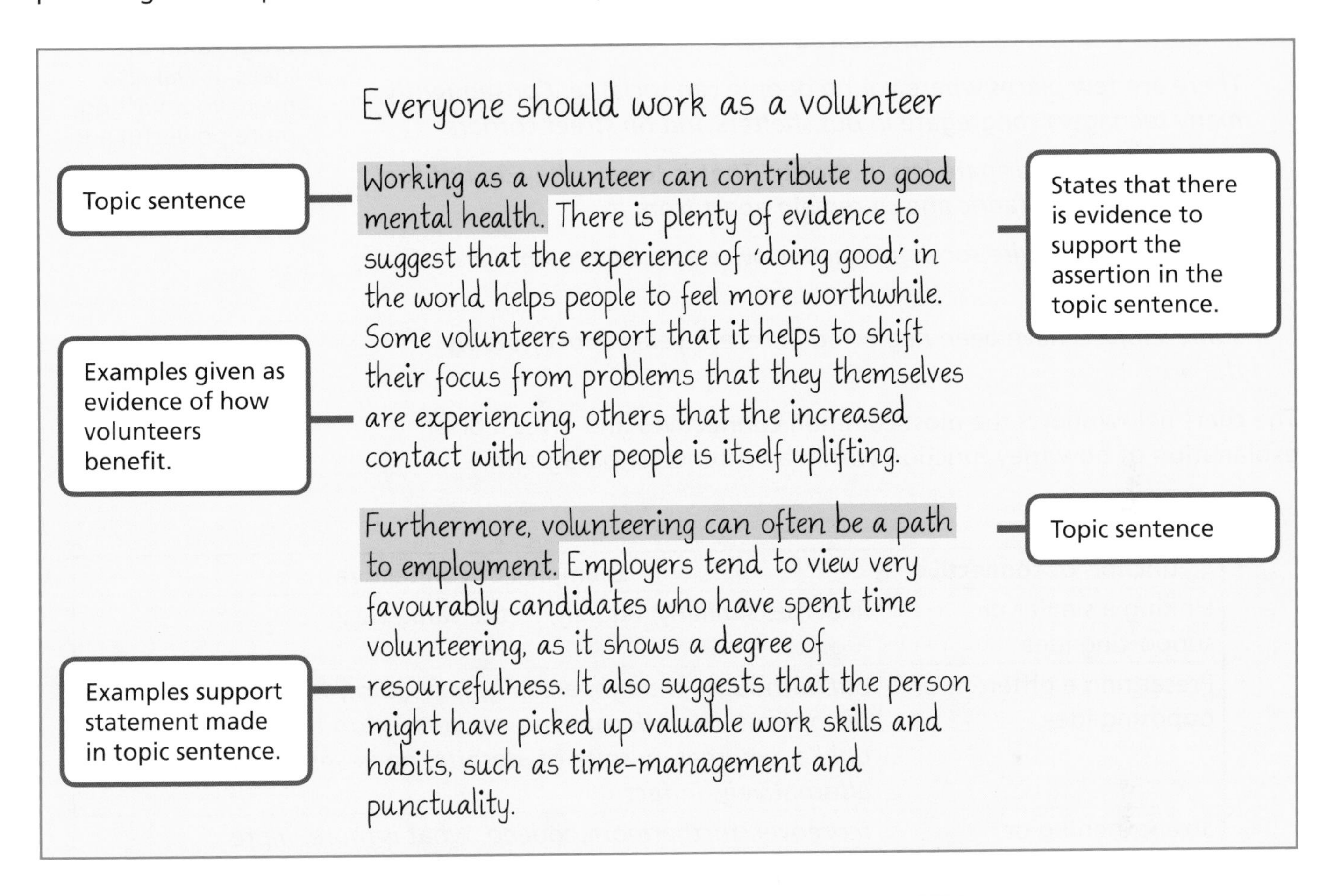

Everyone should work as a volunteer
Topic sentence
Working as a volunteer can contribute to good mental health. There is plenty of evidence to suggest that the experience of 'doing good' in the world helps people to feel more worthwhile. Some volunteers report that it helps to shift their focus from problems that they themselves are experiencing, others that the increased contact with other people is itself uplifting.
States that there is evidence to support the assertion in the topic sentence.
Examples given as evidence of how volunteers benefit.
Furthermore, volunteering can often be a path to employment. Employers tend to view very favourably candidates who have spent time volunteering, as it shows a degree of resourcefulness. It also suggests that the person might have picked up valuable work skills and habits, such as time-management and punctuality.
Topic sentence
Examples support statement made in topic sentence.

PARAGRAPH LENGTH

In persuasive writing, the main paragraphs that form the body of the essay are usually of similar length. In fiction, however, paragraph length tends to vary:

- Short paragraphs – even one-line paragraphs – can have the effect of grabbing the reader's attention and are sometimes used to convey excitement and drama.
- Conversely, long paragraphs can have the effect of slowing down the action. For this reason, they are often used to convey the thoughts and reflections of the **protagonist**, rather than describing action:

I reflected long and hard about my choices. I paced the room waiting for the clock to strike, and checked my own watch.

Then, out of the blue, there was a knock at the door.

TOP TIP 

When you are writing a piece of fiction, vary the length of your paragraphs to produce a text with a more interesting and engaging rhythm.

HOW TO USE CONNECTIVES

Connectives are words and phrases that link ideas within a piece of writing. They perform various functions. For example, some connectives link ideas that are similar ('likewise', 'similarly') and some show contrasts between ideas ('however', 'although'). Other connectives introduce an example of what is being discussed ('such as', 'for instance'). There are many other connectives, with a variety of functions. They may appear in the middle of a sentence or at the start of it:

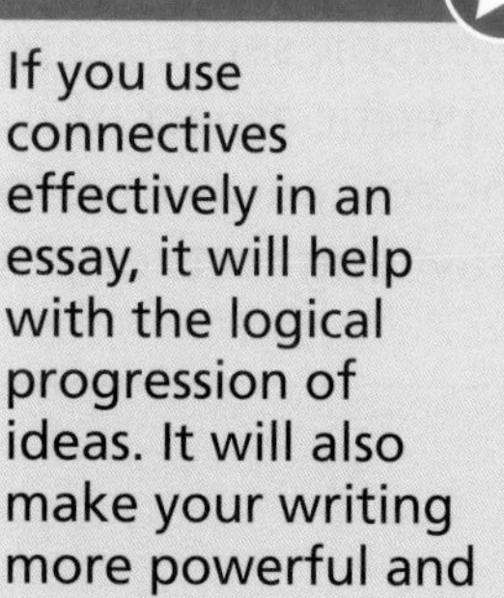

TOP TIP
If you use connectives effectively in an essay, it will help with the logical progression of ideas. It will also make your writing more powerful and persuasive.

> *There are few places where young people can socialise.* ***Consequently,*** *many teenagers congregate in bus shelters and on street corners.*
>
> *These people participate less in society.* ***That is to say,*** *they do not feel part of the social fabric and so remain apart from it.*
>
> *Board games require social interaction* ***whereas*** *video games are often played alone.*
>
> *Some subjects have been neglected in recent years,* ***most notably*** *the arts.*

The chart below shows the most common connectives and gives a brief explanation of how they function within a sentence or paragraph.

Function of connective	Examples of connectives
Linking a similar or supporting idea	*likewise, similarly, equally, in the same way*
Presenting a different or opposing idea	*but, although, though, actually, instead of, in contrast, by way of contrast, in stark contrast, conversely, on the other hand, unlike, whereas, in spite of, despite, however, nevertheless, yet, alternatively, in fact*
Strengthening or developing an argument	*moreover, furthermore, indeed, what is more, more importantly, above all, besides, in addition, first and foremost*
Showing consequences	*consequently, as a consequence, as a result, thus, hence, because of this, inevitably*
Giving reasons	*so, therefore, for this reason, that is why, accordingly*
Giving specific examples	*for example, such as, for instance, notably, most notably, specifically, namely, in particular, in the case of*
Indicating order	*firstly, secondly, thirdly, lastly, finally*
Showing purpose	*for that/this reason, with this in mind, to this end*
Introducing a summary	*to summarise, in summary, to conclude, in conclusion, in brief, in short*
Generalising	*overall, on the whole, in general*
For persuading	*evidently, clearly, surely, certainly, undoubtedly*
Placing in time	*previously, formerly, in the past, at one time, now, nowadays, these days, at this point, currently, later on, subsequently, in future, in time, at once, meanwhile, immediately, straightaway*
Clarifying	*in other words, that is to say*

When a connective is used to start a sentence, it needs a comma after it.

Consequently, *many young people who wish to train for a profession find themselves unable to do so.*

Furthermore, *the practice is damaging to the environment.*

To summarise, *the situation is unsustainable and we must find solutions to it or jeopardise the future of humanity.*

CHECK YOUR SKILLS

1 Read these sentences from a student's persuasive essay. Complete each sentence with one of the connectives from the box. Use each connective only once.

furthermore	unlike	namely	however	as a result

a) *Of course, many older people have engaged with the issues affecting our future.*

.............................., a significant number simply have not.

b) *Young people today are much more politically aware .... of the obligatory 'politics and society' classes that form part of the national syllabus.*

c) *The extension of voting rights to 16-year-olds would acknowledge this greater political engagement. ...., it would actively encourage it, which can only be beneficial to society.*

d) *Many of the older generation are not in a position to take decisions on these matters, ... the well-informed younger generation.*

e) *Indeed many older people even deny the existence of the biggest threat to face our planet, ... climate change.*

TEST YOURSELF

Now complete these tasks to check what you have learnt in Part Five.
You can find the answers in Part Seven.

1. This text is a letter to a local newspaper complaining about an article critical of lazy, antisocial teenagers. It argues that teenagers are not lazy or antisocial and that in fact they contribute a great deal to society.

   Turn the text into **four paragraphs**, indicating with two lines '//' where you would start each new paragraph. Add the **connectives** from the box to make the text flow. Use each connective only once.

for this reason	moreover	lastly	evidently	despite	for instance	firstly

Dear Sir,

I am writing to you to express my outrage at an article 'Alienated teens' printed in February 12th's edition of your newspaper. The whole tone of the article is prejudiced and mean-spirited. ...., it's entirely inaccurate. As a young person of the city, I would very much like to take this opportunity to set the matter straight. ...., I take issue with the journalist's (Andrew Walker) claim that young people 'contribute less to the community than older members'. ...., Mr Walker hasn't met the young people that I spend time with, many of whom give a great deal back to the community! ...., three of my friends work in local charity shops on Saturday, giving up seven hours of their free time .... having heavy college workloads to be fitted in around other commitments. These three young people in no way resemble Walker's 'gangs of alienated teens, hanging around the local shop and littering the pavement'. Other young people of my acquaintance may not work as volunteers, but they are politically engaged, channelling their energies into campaigns and protests. These young people march and raise money for causes that they believe in. They are certainly not the idle, anti-social young people of Andrew Walker's article. All are conscientious, ambitious and hard-working – the teachers, doctors and scientists, etc. of the future. ...., I would like to point out that, whether we approve of them or not, today's youth are the future. .... alone, we should show them some respect, or at least, give them a chance to prove themselves.

Yours faithfully,

Hannah Webb

PROGRESS CHECK FOR PART FIVE

GOOD PROGRESS

I can:

- Use paragraphs appropriately and effectively in creative and persuasive writing ❑
- Use connectives to link paragraphs and to link ideas within sentences ❑

EXCELLENT PROGRESS

I can:

- Use paragraphs appropriately and effectively in creative and persuasive writing and vary the length of paragraphs for stylistic effect ❑
- Use a range of connectives to link paragraphs and to link ideas within sentences ❑

TEST YOURSELF ON ALL THE KEY SKILLS

Now test yourself on everything you have learnt in this book. You can find the answers in Part Seven.

❶ Correct the **spellings** that are wrong. Tick the ones that are correct.

a) allagory ....

b) dialogue ....

c) omnicient ....

d) playright ....

e) euphemism ....

f) repitition ....

g) onomatapoeia ....

h) personification ....

i) technique ....

j) sillable ....

❷ Write the **plural form** of these words.

a) wish ....

b) story ....

c) verse ....

d) echo ....

e) belief ....

f) phenomenon ....

g) quality ....

h) leaf ....

❸ Circle **one word** in each group that would be particularly appropriate for a frightening story.

a) hiss / recite / drawl / purr

b) dewy / wet / clammy / juicy

c) ooze / flow / spout / run

d) bend / squat / cower / kneel

e) eerie / mythical / unusual / eccentric

f) glide / swim / float / slither

❹ Circle the correct word to complete the sentences.

a) '[Whose / Who's] *got the map?' asked James.*

b) *Dad took my sister and* [I / me] *to the ice rink.*

c) *Please let the organisers know if* [your / you're] *going to be late.*

d) *The dog has* [its / it's] *own place to sleep.*

e) *Have you seen* [there / their / they're] *new house?*

f) *That is the man* [who / whom] *gave me the message.*

❺ Complete these sentences with **comparatives** and **superlatives**. Use the adjectives given in brackets.

a) *That was the* .... *exam I've ever done. I'm sure it was* .... *than last year's paper.* (bad, hard)

b) *The first poem is* .... *than the second and is also* .... *to understand.* (descriptive, easy)

c) *I'm a lot* .... *than my sister. London is the* .... *she's ever been!* (adventurous, far)

d) *You would be able to work* .... *if you had a* .... *laptop.* (fast, good)

❻ Some of these sentences contain incorrect grammar. Rewrite each sentence, correcting the grammar. Tick the ones that are correct.

a) *My grandparents lived in Poland when they was younger.*

....

b) *Neither author uses many similes.*

....

c) *His friends should have took him to a doctor.*

....

d) *Jasmine and her friend Laura were late to bed because of the party and hasn't woken up yet.*

....

....

e) *In the morning, there was less snow on the ground.*

....

f) *King Duncan welcomes Macbeth and Banquo and said he would stay at Macbeth's castle.*

....

....

7. Write the **contracted forms** of these words.

   a) does not

   b) I am

   c) she has

   d) would have

   e) they are

   f) had not

8. Add all necessary **punctuation** to these sentences, including capital letters.

   a) *sara and pauls mother who lives in berlin is visiting them next Friday*

   b) *wow gasped rick have you ever seen anything as beautiful as this*

   c) *pramod didnt notice the dark oily water seeping under the door*

   d) *sheers describes the earth as gulping for breath*

   e) *you took the money didnt you the man yelled*

   f) *theres a market on saturdays where you can buy bread vegetables fruit fish and cheese*

   g) *mira jasons mother asked her for information about the journey*

   h) *his parents ideas were rather old-fashioned they wanted him to be a doctor*

9. Look at this excerpt from the middle part of a story. Copy out the excerpt, putting in paragraphs where you think they should begin. Correct any punctuation errors.

> However when we arrived at the cottage there was no sign of Lucy. Inside, the place looked as if it had been ransacked, papers and clothes were strewn all over the floor and crockery smashed. Karls face was ashen. 'We're too late,' he groaned, 'If only we hadnt wasted time looking for the key.' We stood for a while, looking around in bewilderment. What on earth–or who on earth-had caused this scene of devastation! Suddenly I noticed something. 'Look'! I shouted. 'Look over there! Its a message from Lucy. I know it is!' On the table lay a tiny crumpled scrap of paper with a few words hastily scrawled on it. Karl snatched it up and smoothed it out. 'I think,' he announced, 'That we were right all along – and this is the proof!'

....

....

....

....

....

....

....

10 Look at this paragraph from a piece of descriptive writing. Copy out the paragraph, correcting any grammar errors. Suggest replacements for the underlined words and phrases to give the piece more interest and impact.

Her heart hammering, the girl runs quickly through the bleak forest, arms and legs waving in her panic. Trees crowd in from every side, reaching out with there bare limbs as if to trap her. A small amount of sunshine comes through the trees, reflecting on the icy grass. Fallen branches lie like whitened bones on the forest floor and the hard, uneven path threaten to trip her at every step. She is becoming more and more tireder but she knows that the loud footsteps of the two men behind her is getting closer. Fear was her only source of energy. She can not let them catch her. She knows only too well that neither man have any pity.

11 Read this excerpt from a critical analysis of Thomas Hardy's poem 'Neutral Tones'. Copy out the excerpt on a separate piece of paper, correcting any **spelling errors**.

Hardy uses imagary connected with the season of winter. The coldness of the winter's day and the description of the dead leaves serve as a metapher for the relationship that is the subject of the poem. For example, he describes the sun as 'white' and 'God-curst', in contrast to our usual perseption of it as warm and life-giving. In the first stanza, he also describes the 'starving sod', showing us that this is an enviroment in which nothing can grow, including love. His ommission of the word 'tree' after 'ash' is also striking because it makes us consious of the other meaning of ash – the substanse that remains after something has been burned. These descriptions of the pond and its surroundings have the affect of creating a sense of unease before we reach the second stanza, in which he begins to talk about the other person in the relationship.

⓬ Look at this paragraph from a viewpoint essay about the pros and cons of wearing a school uniform. Add a **topic sentence** at the beginning of the paragraph, then correct any **grammar, spelling** or **punctuation errors**. Write the corrected passage on the lines below.

> [Topic sentence] Although pupils always try to find ways of getting round the rules – shorter skirts, better-cut trousers, etc. – there is limits to how far they can go. One pupils coat may be slightly more trendier than another's or there may be some differences in the style of shoes, the differences will not be great. This means that pupils from the poorest family's do not look fundamentally different than those from the richest, which I beleive is a good thing. Pupils at schools without uniforms can easy get drawn into a fashion competition, which is a waste of money time and effort.

13 Now read and complete this longer task, following the proofreading guidance below.

Write the opening part of a story that is set in a dangerous place.

As you write, and once you have finished, proofread your work for the following points. You could use a grid like the one shown below.

- **Spelling:** Think about words that often cause problems, for instance 'it's' and 'its', or words that sound similar, such as 'effect' and 'affect'.
- **Grammar:** Make sure your tenses are consistent and that the verb-subject agreement is correct.
- **Punctuation:** Check every comma and ask yourself if it should really be a full stop or a conjunction. Make sure that all proper nouns have capital letters and that other nouns do not. Check punctuation for speech.
- **Sentence forms:** Make sure you have used a variety of sentence forms, especially in creative writing. For example, could you add a minor sentence or a rhetorical question for dramatic effect?
- **Paragraphs:** Make sure that your paragraphs are not too long and that they reflect the structure of the content. Check that you have used appropriate connectives and added commas after words such as 'However, ...'
- **Vocabulary:** Check for repetition of words and think about whether you could replace any words with ones that are more interesting or have more impact.

Elements to check	Key things to look out for	As I go along	At the end
Spelling	Words that often cause problems, such as "it's" and "its"; words that sound similar, such as "effect" and "affect"	✓	✓
Grammar	Make sure tenses are consistent		
Punctuation			

When you proofread, try to make your corrections as neat as possible:

- For spelling mistakes, cross out the incorrect spelling and write the correct one above. It is usually clearer to correct the whole word rather than just one or two letters in it. You are not allowed to use correction fluids, pens or tape in exams.
- If you have missed out a word, write the symbol ^ where it should go, and write the word above the line. For a longer phrase or sentence, write an asterisk (*) where it should go, and an asterisk with the missing words at the end of the piece of writing.
- To split a paragraph, write // where the new paragraph starts.

ANSWERS

PART TWO: SPELLINGS FOR SUCCESS

SPELLING STRATEGIES [pp. 15–18]

4 Check your skills

a) repetition / assonance

b) similes

c) Admittedly

d) undoubtedly

e) notably / narrator

f) soliloquys / protagonist

g) contradict

h) therefore

i) analogous

j) foreboding

LETTER ORDER AND SILENT LETTERS [pp. 19–21]

1

a) achieve

b) ✓

c) receive

d) ✓

e) ✓

f) foreign

g) ✓

h) ✓

i) protein

j) ✓

2

a) playwrights

b) knot

c) whole

d) whistles

e) rhyme

f) bustle

g) numb

3

a) wreaked

b) campaign

c) knelt

d) conscious

e) knowledge

f) scene

g) rustle/rustled

h) campaign

i) reign

j) playwright

UNDERSTANDING PLURALS [p. 24]

1

It was seven o'clock in the morning and bitterly cold when Rebecca set off. She turned left at the end of the road and walked towards the stream. The ***roofs*** *of the houses that she passed sparkled with frost and the* ***leaves*** *under her feet crunched as she stepped on them. She loved this time of year. It brought back so many happy* ***memories*** *of playing with her younger brother in the back garden, wrapped snuggly in* ***scarves****, their cheeks as red as* ***tomatoes****.*

She thought of her brother, Ali, as she crossed the road to join the path beside the stream. They would come here in the summer, when the air was buzzing with ***flies****. Ali used to love delving in the water with his net, trying – and always failing – to catch a fish. There were no fish this morning – they were presumably keeping warm at the bottom of the stream. The other side of the stream, there was a small wooded area. She would take her brother there, his plump, trusting hand in hers. Once, just once, she had told him that there were* ***wolves*** *in the wood and he had cried and begged to be taken home. She hadn't meant to upset him, just to inject a little excitement into their walk.*

PREFIXES AND SUFFIXES [p. 27]

1 Check your skills

a) shriek

b) conceited

c) doubt

d) wolves

e) echoes

f) women

g) accept

h) bear

i) cheerful

j) disservice

TEST YOURSELF [pp. 28–29]

1

a) argument

b) privilege

c) relevant

d) protagonist

e) accommodation

f) liaison

g) separate

h) parliament

i) contradict

j) disappointed

k) misspell

l) coping

2

a) envir**on**ment

b) station**ary**

c) independ**en**t

d) monolo**gue**

e) onomato**poeia**

f) perc**ei**ves

g) **a**ffected

h) hopeful

3

a) women

b) crises

c) phenomena

d) parentheses

e) criteria

f) analyses

4

My lungs feel as if they are about to burst as I turn into the final straight. With the 25th mile marker ***past*** *me, my* ***doubts*** *are all behind me. For the first time in the race, I know I am going to make it. Finally, I'm going to* ***fulfil*** *my ambition. I force myself to put one blistered and bloodied foot in front of another. Not long to go now – I can do it.*

The agony of the last ten miles – a ***persistent*** *cramp in both* ***calves*** *– is at last receding and a welcome* ***numbness*** *spreads upwards through my legs. Indeed, I can scarcely feel them now. Will they even* ***bear*** *my weight? I look down at them –* ***familiar****, and yet strangely alien, these appendages that seem to move of their own accord, as if* ***independent*** *of me. The relief, though, is beyond words. In fact, I have no words – no thoughts, even. All I have is focus, one single focus – I must reach that finishing line. Crowds stand at the roadside, cheering and urging us on but I am scarcely* ***conscious*** *of them. I must keep going.*

The finish line finally comes into view and I feel a sudden surge of energy and joy – ***ecstasy*** *even. This is the moment my* ***whole*** *being has been going towards. I marshal every last ounce of energy and determination to accomplish this one goal. I focus on the finishing line as if my life depends on it and force my body onwards.*

PART THREE: GET YOUR GRAMMAR RIGHT!

VOCABULARY FOR IMPACT [p. 31]

1

a) X

b) N

c) N

d) P

e) P

f) N

2

a) X

b) N

c) N

d) P

e) P

f) P

3 Check your skills

Example answers:

a) Rain lashed down and soaked into our clothes.

b) The menacing peaks towered above us.

c) I let the beautiful, soothing music flow over me.

WHAT ARE WORD CLASSES? [pp. 33–35]

1

a) yours, it

b) him, himself

c) whose, them

2

Example answers:

a) 'You're so lucky!' Jan said **enviously/jealously**, staring around at Hugo's **plush/luxurious** apartment.

b) Having studied so **hard/conscientiously**, Philip was **totally/utterly** devastated to fail the exam.

c) Her **chestnut/luxuriant** hair fell in waves to her waist, gleaming as she moved **gracefully/slowly** towards us.

3

In my opinion, whether or not celebrities can be true role models depends ***on*** *why they are famous. A sportsperson or a musician* ***whose*** *skills inspire ordinary people can be a worthy role model, but this is very different* ***from*** *admiring someone merely for* ***their*** *wealth or lifestyle.*

However, in general I believe that our society would benefit from choosing role models with ***humbler/ more humble*** *qualities such as kindness and generosity. If* ***fewer*** *people aspired to wealth and celebrity, I believe we could achieve a* ***better*** *society for everyone.*

CLAUSES AND TYPES OF SENTENCES [p. 37]

1

a) simple sentence 3

b) compound sentence 1, 5

c) complex sentence 2

d) minor sentence 4

USING SENTENCES ACCURATELY AND EFFECTIVELY [p. 39]

1

Example answer:

I woke up with a start and looked around. Where was James? Then I realised that the jewels and all my money had gone! I can barely describe how I felt at that moment – angry, scared and utterly betrayed. The worst thing was that I had trusted James. What a fool I was!

SUBJECT AND VERB AGREEMENT [pp. 40–41]

1

a) has

b) is

c) describes

2 Check your skills

a) In the novel, everyone they encounter **tries** to thwart their efforts.

b) She does not believe that any of the servants is trustworthy. ✓

c) There is no use of similes in the poem. ✓

d) I do not feel that either author **succeeds** in capturing the atmosphere of a fair.

e) Everybody in the room **has** some connection with the dead woman.

USING TENSES CONSISTENTLY [p. 43]

1 Check your skills

write **wrote** written

catch caught **caught**

choose **chose** chosen

fly **flew** flown

forgive forgave **forgiven**

hurt hurt **hurt**

throw **threw** thrown

2

a) Jack's father **came** back to the house because he had **forgotten** his umbrella.

b) Susie **did** the cooking yesterday, so I **will do it/am going to do it/am doing it** today.

c) The thieves **broke** into the house while Anna **was sleeping**.

THE POWER OF MODAL VERBS [p. 45]

Example answers:

1 Check your skills

a) *In my opinion, the government should ban smoking completely. Smoking can cause many serious diseases and our hospitals may soon be unable to cope with the increasing demands on their services.*

b) *The government has already banned smoking in public buildings, but it should have done more. Seeing adults smoke in any situation can encourage children to take up the habit.*

c) *Smokers might argue that they have a right to smoke, but if they insist on that right, we may have to consider charging them extra for health care.*

TEST YOURSELF [pp. 46–47]

1

hideous, grotesque, ghastly (e.g. repulsive, monstrous, horrible)

immaculate, ideal, flawless (e.g. faultless, perfect, impeccable)

serene, unruffled, placid (e.g. tranquil, calm)

wretched, miserable, heartbroken (e.g. despondent, sorrowful, unhappy)

2

a) We saw a ruined castle on top of a hill.

b) Rob loved swimming, although he had to get up very early to practise. / Although he had to get up very early to practise, Rob loved swimming. / Although Rob had to get up very early to practise, he loved swimming.

c) One girl distracted the man while the other girl stole his passport. / While one girl distracted the man, the other girl stole his passport.

d) There was a huge crowd of tourists.

e) Maria and Charlie play the piano but Rory doesn't.

3

Noun: year, Marilyn

Pronoun: me, mine

Verb: remember, reckon

Adjective: glamorous, bold

Adverb: extremely, heavily

Preposition: at, from

Conjunction: and, or

Determiner: those, my

4

a) We cannot be sure whether either character **is** telling the truth.

b) Meena steals sweets from a shop but **is** caught by her father. [or **stole**]

c) None of the children remember their father. ✓

d) Macbeth is reassured by the witches' prophecies because he knows that trees cannot move. ✓

e) He is happy because Anna has **forgiven** him.

5

*Sometimes **it is/it's** easy to feel that everyone expects us to be perfect. We think that if only we **were** prettier, cleverer or more popular, life would be **easier** and we would have **fewer** problems. It's not surprising if these high expectations **cause** stress.*

*The first thing to say is don't **worry. Stress** is a normal part of life, but if **you're** feeling really bad, the **worst** thing you can do is bottle up your feelings, so find someone to talk to.*

6

Example answer:

A true eccentric. That's what my parents used to call our neighbour, the ancient Mrs Hobson. She'd once been a singer, they told me. To me, however, Mrs Hobson was a witch – a scary, bird-like figure with gnarled hands and a wizened face. I hated her cackling voice and the nauseating smell of stew that came from her kitchen. Even so, there was no excuse for what I did to her that day. None at all.

PART FOUR: PUNCTUATION FOR ACCURACY AND EFFECT

FULL STOPS, QUESTION MARKS AND EXCLAMATION MARKS [p. 49]

1 Check your skills

*I was on holiday in France with my family. Mum and Dad were sunbathing on the beach. **M**y brother and I were playing at the water's edge, letting the waves knock us over. **S**uddenly, I saw a giant wave coming towards us. **I**t was as high as a house! **I**t crashed over us and I could feel myself being sucked underneath it. **W**as this it? **W**as I going to die?*

COMMAS [pp. 50–51]

1

a) Dr Jekyll**,** who wants to suppress his evil impulses**,** creates a potion to help him do this.

b) Moreover**,** homework**,** which can take up a lot of a pupil's time**,** has not been proved to be beneficial.

c) However**,** uniforms can enforce a sense of discipline in school.

2 Check your skills

Although it was midday, a strange silence had descended. The street below my apartment, usually so bustling and cheerful, was deserted. I peered anxiously out of the window, unable to make sense of my surroundings. The whole city seemed to be permeated with a ghostly, yellowish light.

Cars were still and abandoned, shops had their shutters down and even the dogs had stopped their barking.

I went into my room and took out a suitcase. Clothes, toothbrush, passport. I knew I had to get away.

BRACKETS AND DASHES [pp. 52–53]

1

a) Make sure you bring walking boots, a drink (**in** a flask), a map and binoculars.

b) We tried a variety of activities (climbing, abseiling and archery) on the course.

c) He received a letter from [**the** boy's father].

2 Check your skills

a) If students experience physical symptoms of stress (racing heartbeat, dizziness, etc.), they should see the college nurse.

b) Hastie Lanyon – once a close friend of Jekyll – is a very respectable doctor.

c) Children in the 3–6 age group may not yet have learnt sufficient self-control.

APOSTROPHES [pp. 54–55]

1

a) Meena and her friend take the Rutters' poodle to Dale End Farm.

b) Anita and Meena go to each other's houses.

c) Anita and Meena are chased by dogs, and Meena loses her mother's diamond necklace.

d) Sam and Anita's taunting messages distract Meena from her revision.

2 Check your skills

a) I'm late for school, so it'd be great if you'd give me a lift.

b) We didn't see Ed because he'd already left before we arrived.

c) I don't know who's coming to the meeting we've organised.

d) We'll go for a walk later if the weather's good.

COLONS AND SEMICOLONS [p. 57]

1 Check your skills

a) Meena's parents are from a region on the India–Pakistan border. In India, Hindus were in the majority; in Pakistan, most of the population was Muslim. (because there is contrast between the clauses)

b) Shelley's poem 'Ozymandias' is about the ephemeral nature of power: the ruined statue contrasts starkly with its arrogant inscription. (because it is adding an example to support the first sentence)

c) In the town, it was a morning like any other: harassed commuters rushed from the station; in the market, traders were setting up their stalls; tourists paused a moment to take in the scene (colon because extra information is added; semicolons to divide long items in a list)

EFFECTIVE SPEECH PUNCTUATION [p. 59]

1

a) 'Let me help you,' she offered. 'It's too much work for you to do alone.'

b) 'I have never,' Catherine declared, 'seen anything like this before.'

c) The young man told us that he was lost.

d) Kira asked, 'Who is in charge here?'

2 Check your skills

Example answer:

'This is it!' said Ben. 'This is the cave I was telling you about.'

'Wow! How did you find it?' asked Freddy.

'Do you remember the old book I found in the log cabin?'

'The one the old man wrote?'

'Yes,' Ben said. 'It had a map in it, and instructions about how to get down to the shore.'

TEST YOURSELF [pp. 60–61]

1

a) 'It's unfair, isn't it**?'** Sophie complained. 'Mum won't let us go with her.'

b) He cycled over 200 (that's two *hundred*!) miles a day.

c) 'Arnie's never had a pizza**!'** Joel exclaimed.

d) Can this trend be reversed**?** Experts say that it can, but only with difficulty.

2

Example answers:

a) Harri's relationship with the English language is complex: English is the official language of Ghana but many words are still unfamiliar.

b) Daniel was confident but his brother was very shy.

c) The texts are very different. The first author uses a lot of description; the second author has a much plainer style.

3

a) Macbeth wonders if the witches' prophecy **–** that he will become king **–** could be true. (round brackets are also possible)

b) Kelman suggests that children **–** whether native or immigrant **–** had terrible lives in Britain. (round brackets are also possible)

c) The excursion **(**paid for by Laurie's father**)** was a great success. (dashes with spaces are also possible)

4

a) Heaney uses the adjective **'**wizened**'** to describe the earth.

b) Meena resents the Aunties' interference in her life. ✓

c) 'You'll need this,**'** Dexter said.

d) The man asked us where we were from**.**

e) 'You're right,' Carrie agreed. 'We need help.' ✓

5

Example answer:

I woke up with a start. ***T****here was a hammering noise coming from the other side of the wall.*

*'Wake up, Hettie!' I hissed at my sister. 'There****'s*** *someone in Dad's study.'*

'Oh no!' she said, climbing out of bed.

We walked across the cold, bare floorboards and out onto the landing. Everything was quiet: even the wind had stopped its howling.

*Hettie****,*** *who is never usually scared****,*** *looked pale.*

'I've just remembered,' she whispered, ***'w****hat that man on the horse told us. He was right, wasn't he?'*

*I froze. Could it really be true****?*** *Could the thing we'd been dreading for so long really be happening?*

6

Example answer:

In conclusion, I feel that the advantages of TV outweigh the disadvantages. Although many children watch too much TV, this is really their parents' responsibility, not that of the TV companies. Many children's programmes are educational and adults can learn from TV too, with documentaries, news programmes and even dramas which introduce them to new concepts. Moreover, TV is not only about education – relaxation and entertainment are important elements of an enjoyable life too.

PART FIVE: PARAGRAPHS AND ORGANISATION

USING PARAGRAPHS EFFECTIVELY [p. 63]

1

Claudia hadn't really looked at him properly before. She'd acquired a general impression of him, but that was all. Now, in the bright winter light, she regarded him and took in the details – the set of his square jaw, the sprinkling of grey hairs at the temple. He was what most people would describe as handsome. // 'So when are you leaving?' he enquired. // 'Next week,' she replied. 'It's suddenly so close! I still have so much packing to do.' // 'Well, good luck with it all.' // 'Yes, thanks!' // His eye was suddenly drawn to the young man behind her, who he then hailed with a friendly 'Hey!'. Their conversation was over. // That evening, as she surveyed the untidy mound of unpacked boxes, she reflected on her brief conversation with her soon-to-be ex-neighbour. Why had she felt so awkward? Why hadn't she been able to think of anything amusing or interesting to say? What a missed opportunity!

HOW TO USE CONNECTIVES [p. 67]

1 Check your skills

a) However

b) as a result

c) Furthermore

d) unlike

e) namely

TEST YOURSELF [p. 68]

1

I am writing to you to express my outrage at an article 'Alienated teens' printed in February 12th's edition of your newspaper. The whole tone of the article is prejudiced and mean-spirited. ***Moreover****, it's entirely inaccurate. As a young person of the city, I would very much like to take this opportunity to set the matter straight. //* ***First****, I take issue with the journalist's (Andrew Walker) claim that young people 'contribute less to the community than older members'.* ***Evidently****, Mr Walker hasn't met the young people that I spend time with, many of whom give a great deal back to the community!* ***For instance****, three of my friends work in local charity shops on Saturday, giving up seven hours of their free time* ***despite*** *having heavy college workloads to be fitted in around other commitments. These three young people in no way resemble Walker's 'gangs of alienated teens, hanging around the local shop and littering the pavement'. // Other young people of my acquaintance may not work as volunteers, but they are politically engaged, channelling their energies into campaigns and protests. These young people march and raise money for causes that they believe in. They are certainly not the idle, anti-social young people of Andrew Walker's article. All are conscientious, ambitious and hard-working – the teachers, doctors and scientists, etc. of the future. //* ***Lastly****, I would like to point out that, whether we approve of them or not, today's youth are the future.* ***For this reason*** *alone, we should show them some respect, or at least, give them a chance to prove themselves.*

Yours faithfully,

Hannah Webb

PART SIX: TEST YOURSELF

TEST YOURSELF [p. 70–75]

1

a) allegory

b) ✓

c) omniscient

d) playwright

e) ✓

f) repetition

g) onomatopoeia

h) ✓

i) ✓

j) syllable

2

a) wishes

b) stories

c) verses

d) echoes

e) beliefs

f) phenomena

g) qualities

h) leaves

3

a) hiss

b) clammy

c) ooze

d) cower

e) eerie

f) slither

4

a) Who's

b) me

c) you're

d) its

e) their

f) who

5

a) worst, harder

b) more descriptive, easier

c) more adventurous, furthest

d) faster, better

6

a) My grandparents lived in Poland when they **were** younger.

b) ✓

c) His friends should have **taken** him to a doctor.

d) Jasmine and her friend Laura were late to bed because of the party and **haven't** woken up yet.

e) ✓

f) King Duncan welcomes Macbeth and Banquo and **says** he **will** stay at Macbeth's castle.

7

a) doesn't

b) I'm

c) she's

d) would've

e) they're

f) hadn't

8

a) Sara and Paul's mother, who lives in Berlin, is visiting them next Friday.

b) 'Wow!' gasped Rick. 'Have you ever seen anything as beautiful as this?'

c) Pramod didn't notice the dark, oily water seeping under the door.

d) Sheers describes the earth as 'gulping for breath'.

e) 'You took the money, didn't you?' the man yelled.

f) There's a market on Saturdays where you can buy bread, vegetables, fruit, fish and cheese

g) Mira (Jason's mother) asked her for information about the journey.

h) His parents' ideas were rather old-fashioned. They wanted him to be a doctor.

9

However**,** when we arrived at the cottage there was no sign of Lucy. Inside, the place looked as if it had been ransacked**. Papers** [*or* **ransacked: papers**] and clothes were strewn all over the floor and crockery smashed. **Karl's** face was ashen.

'We're too late,' he groaned**.** 'If only we **hadn't** wasted time looking for the key.'

We stood for a while, looking around in bewilderment. What on earth – or who on earth – had caused this scene of devastation**?**

Suddenly I noticed something.

'Look**!**' I shouted. 'Look over there! **It's** a message from Lucy. I know it is!' On the table lay a tiny**,** crumpled scrap of paper with a few words hastily scrawled on it. Karl snatched it up and smoothed it out.

'I think,' he announced, '**that** we were right all along – and this is the proof!'

10 (Vocabulary changes are suggestions)

Her heart hammering, the girl **races frantically** through the bleak forest, arms and legs **flailing/ thrashing wildly** in her panic. Trees crowd in from every side, reaching out with **their** bare limbs as if to trap her. **Cold sunshine filters weakly** through the trees, reflecting on the icy grass. Fallen branches lie like whitened bones on the forest floor and the hard, uneven path **threatens** to trip her at every step. She is becoming more and more **tired** but she knows that the **thundering** footsteps of the two men behind her **are** getting closer. Fear **is** her only source of energy. She **cannot** let them catch her. She knows only too well that neither man **has** any pity.

11

Hardy uses **imagery** connected with the season of winter. The coldness of the winter's day and the description of the dead leaves serve as a **metaphor** for the relationship that is the subject of the poem. For example, he describes the sun as 'white' and 'God-curst', in contrast to our usual **perception** of it as warm and life-giving. In the first stanza, he also describes the 'starving sod', showing us that this is an **environment** in which nothing can grow, including love. His **omission** of the word 'tree' after 'ash' is also striking, because it makes us **conscious** of the other meaning of ash – the **substance** that remains after something has been burned. These descriptions of the pond and its surroundings have the **effect** of creating a sense of unease before we reach the second stanza, in which he begins to talk about the other person in the relationship.

12

School uniforms are a way of making all pupils equal. Although pupils always try to find ways of getting round the rules – shorter skirts, better-cut trousers, etc. – there **are** limits to how far they can go. One **pupil's** coat may be slightly **trendier** than another's or there may be some differences in the style of **shoes but** the differences will not be great. This means that pupils from the poorest **families** do not look fundamentally different **from** those from the richest, which I **believe** is a good thing. Pupils at schools without uniforms can **easily** get drawn into a fashion competition, which is a waste of money**,** time and effort.

13

Example answer:

A variety of sentence forms are used. Simple sentences are used for impact **[1]**, and are contrasted with compound and complex sentences in more descriptive passages. **[6]** A minor sentence emphasises the narrator's shock. **[10]**

The present tense adds a sense of immediacy and subject-verb agreement is correct. **[5]**

Paragraph lengths are varied for effect, including one-sentence paragraphs at the beginning. **[1]** Paragraphs match the content – new paragraphs introduce new ideas. **[7]**

This isn't possible.

This can't be happening. **[1]**

I'm cold, cold, cold. My eyes are sore. There's **[2]** *a roaring noise in the dark air above me:* **[3]** *a screaming and groaning as if a thousand angry spirits are swooping together in a whirlwind of fury.* **[4]**

I know that the rushing and shrieking in the treetops is just wind, but no matter how much I know it, I don't feel it. **[5]** *When I open my eyes and look up, I see thin, leafy branches thrashing above me. When I close them, I see flying creatures with huge, dark eye sockets, grinning mouths with rotten teeth, the cloth of tattered white cloaks streaming behind them.* **[6]**

The skin on my face is stiff from the salt of my tears and my mouth tastes disgusting, but my eyes are getting heavier and heavier and I rest my head back against the tree trunk.

[7] *Now I can see Aunty Nina's* **[8]** *face. She's bending over me and asking me if my arm is broken. I tell her that it isn't, and I smile to myself, comforted that she's there.*

Aunty Nina isn't smiling though.

'Be careful, Scarlett,' she whispers. 'There are snakes in the forest.' **[9]**

Forest! **[10]** *I jump awake again, heart hammering, gasping for breath, trying desperately to work out where I am. For a split second my treacherous brain conjures up my bedroom at home, with the soft glow of my nightlight and Big Panda sitting in the wicker armchair by the window.*

Forest? That's ridiculous. How could I be all alone in the middle of a forest in the middle of the night? **[11]**

I am though. The realisation is like a thud in the pit of my stomach. That's no nightlight – that's a cold sliver of moon above the trees. I'm not lying on a mattress, but a heap of rather slimy, rather smelly leaves. That isn't the window frame – it's just the branches I've pulled over me to make a barrier. That isn't my wicker chair – **[12]** *it's a horrible, prickly* **[13]** *bush that scratched my legs as I made my way in here earlier.*

A wide range of vocabulary is used, including interesting words that add impact. **[4]** Spellings are correct.

A good range of punctuation is used, including a colon to add information **[3]**, correct punctuation of speech **[9]**, dashes to add information **[12]**, commas between adjectives **[13]**, apostrophes for contractions **[2]** and possession **[8]**, an exclamation mark **[10]**, and question marks **[11]**. Capital letters are used where required. **[8]**

Rhetorical questions emphasise the narrator's sense of confusion. **[11]**

GLOSSARY

abstract noun a noun that refers to feelings, concepts or states that do not exist physically (e.g. hope, love)

adjective a word used to describe something or somebody (e.g. 'the **red** hat')

adverb a word used to modify a verb, adjective or another adverb, sometimes formed by adding 'ly' to an adjective

adverbial phrase a phrase that functions like an adverb

antonym a word that has the opposite meaning of another word in the same language

auxiliary verb verbs such as 'be', 'do', 'have'; also modal verbs, which express possibility or necessity: 'must', 'shall', 'will', 'could', 'should', 'would', 'can', 'may' and 'might'

clause a special phrase whose head is a verb; a clause can be a complete sentence

colon (:) a punctuation mark that precedes a list or an expansion in a sentence, or when a character speaks in a play script

comma splice an error of punctuation in which a comma is used to link two independent clauses

comparative adjective an adjective that is used to compare things, such as 'longer', 'darker' or 'more beautiful'

complex sentence a sentence usually made up of a main clause and one or more subordinate clauses

compound sentence a sentence made up of two independent clauses joined by a coordinating conjunction

concrete noun a word for things you can detect with your senses – for example, water, arm, zebra

conjunction a word that links two words or phrases together; there are two types: coordinating conjunctions and subordinating conjunctions

connective a word such as 'however' or 'moreover', used to link paragraphs and show the relationship between them

contraction a word that is made by omitting a letter or letters, for example, 'don't'

coordinating conjunction a conjunction that links two words or phrases together as an equal pair

countable noun a noun such as 'poet', 'character' or 'simile' that can have 'a' or 'an' in front of it, and can be made plural

dash (–) a punctuation mark used to set off a word or phrase after an independent clause

determiner a word that specifies a noun as known or unknown (e.g. 'the', 'a', 'this', 'my', 'some')

dialogue speech and conversation between characters

direct speech words that are actually spoken by a character in a novel or story

ellipsis (...) a series of dots to show where words have been deliberately left out of a sentence ('ellipses' is the plural)

indirect speech words used to report what someone said

inverted comma one of a pair of marks ' ' or " ", used in written language for showing what someone said

main clause a sentence contains at least one main clause, which makes sense on its own

minor sentence a sentence that is grammatically incomplete, perhaps not containing a subject or verb

modal verb a verb such as 'can', 'could', 'may', 'shall', etc. that is used with another verb to express probability, permission, ability, advice or obligation

mood the tone or atmosphere created by an artistic work

mnemonic a memory aid that can help with remembering spelling, for example

noun phrase a word or a group of words used as a noun

part of speech a type of word – for example, a noun, verb, adjective or pronoun

past participle the form of a verb with '-ed' on the end that is used in perfect tenses and the passive structure

phrase a group of words that are grammatically connected

prefix a letter or a group of letters added to the end of a word or letters, which alters its grammatical form and sometimes its meaning ('**aero**plane', '**il**legal')

preposition a word that tells the reader the relationship between things or people, such as 'near', 'by', 'under', 'towards', etc.

pronoun a word that is used instead of a noun (e.g. 'it', 'they', 'this', 'she', 'him')

proper noun a name for things like people, places, historical events, organisations, days and months

protagonist the main or a major character

quotation marks a pair of marks ' ' or " ", used in written language for showing what someone said

relative clause part of a sentence, usually beginning with 'who', 'which', or 'that', that gives information about a person, thing or situation

rhetorical question a question asked for effect, rather than to elicit an answer

root form the most basic form of a word

round brackets () used to include extra information or an afterthought

run-on sentence an error of punctuation in which clauses that should form two or more sentences are written together with no punctuation

semicolon (;) a type of punctuation that links two ideas, events or pieces of information

sentence fragment a sentence in which a necessary part of the sentence (for example, the subject or the verb) is missing

simple sentence a sentence with one main clause, usually containing a subject, verb and object

square brackets ([ ]) a form of punctuation mainly used to enclose words not said by the original speaker or writer to clarify (e.g. *He [the red fox] slipped away, unseen.*)

subject the person or thing that does the action of a verb

subordinate clause a clause that is secondary to another part of the sentence

subordinating conjunction a conjunction that introduces a subordinate clause

suffix a letter or a group of letters added to the end of a word or letters, which alters its grammatical form ('sweet**ness**', 'advent**ure**')

superlative adjective an adjective that is used to show that something or someone has the most of a particular quality, such as 'best', 'cleverest' or 'most ridiculous'

syllable one of the parts into which a word can be divided; it usually contains a vowel

synonym a word that has the same meaning as another word in the same language

tense the way verbs are used to show the time (past, present or future) that the writer is talking about

theme an idea running through a work of literature or art

tone *See mood*

topic sentence a sentence that expresses the main idea of a paragraph; sometimes the first sentence of the paragraph

uncountable noun a noun such as 'poetry', 'imagery' or 'personification' that cannot have 'a' or 'an' in front of it and cannot be made plural

word class a type of word – for example, a noun, verb, adjective or pronoun